Skills in Advanced Biology

Volume 3

Investigating

J W Garvin BSc DipEd DMS CBiol MIBiol

Lecturer in Education (Biosciences), The Schools of Education and
Biology & Biochemistry, The Queen's University of Belfast

Stanley Thornes (Publishers) Ltd

First published in 1995 by:
Stanley Thornes (Publishers) Ltd
Ellenborough House
Wellington Street
CHELTENHAM
GL50 1YW
England

A catalogue record of this book is available from the British Library.

ISBN 0-7487-2048-0

Additional artwork by Peters & Zubransky (UK) Ltd and Barking Dog Art
Typeset by Columns Design and Production Services Ltd, Reading, Berks
Printed and bound in Great Britain at the Bath Press

Also available:
Skills in Advanced Biology
   Volume 1: Dealing with Data (0 8595 0588 X)
   Worksheet Masters (0 8595 0589 8)
   Volume 2: Observing, Recording and Interpreting (0 8595 0817 X)
   Teacher's Supplement (0 7487 0043 9)

To my parents who gave me curious genes
and the environment to express them.

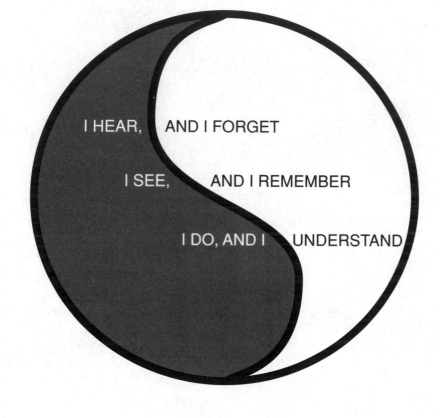

I HEAR,   AND I FORGET

I SEE,   AND I REMEMBER

I DO, AND I   UNDERSTAND

Contents

Preface

To the teacher/lecturer

As a result of changes that have occurred in science courses with the introduction of GCSE and the National Curriculum, changes are inevitably taking place at GCE Advanced level and equivalents. The Government is keen not only to retain A- and AS-levels, but to link post-16 academic and vocational courses. We are moving therefore towards courses which concentrate more and more on the development of skills, especially those skills which are transferable to the outside world of work.

Along with the changes in the examinations, more and more students are staying on to study A-levels and their equivalents, with the inevitable result that the ability range is widening and the variety of subjects studied with biology is tending to increase. In tandem with these changes is the unprecedented increase in the numbers of students entering tertiary education who come from a much wider range of access courses, bringing with them considerable variability both in knowledge and in skills.

This series of skill-based active learning volumes has been designed to address this problem: these books should not be considered as textbooks or even courses – they contain materials which can be used as flexible resources to be incorporated as you see fit into your courses, or for students to use as they wish. The three volumes – 1. *Dealing with Data*; 2. *Observing, Recording and Interpreting*; and 3. *Investigating* – are a synergic whole. Volumes 1 and 2 contain materials that can be incorporated into any A-level biology or introductory tertiary course. They do not require prior knowledge as they mainly consist of procedures whereby the skills are learned using examples, and then applied using exercises.

Volume 3 – Investigating

There is a growing consensus of opinion that A-levels and other courses are too concerned with learning facts. Students should instead be developing the ability to think as biologists and to learn a core of basic skills, central of which is investigating. After they complete their courses, students will need to understand and apply knowledge which has not yet been discovered, and to solve problems continually no matter what their further education or work involves.

The Schools Examination and Assessment Council lists among their principles (as required by all syllabuses):

Promote the study of associated techniques, methods of investigation and applications.

Encourage attitudes of curiosity and enquiry.

Understanding and skills.

Extended pieces of individual work.

Foster different styles of learning, and encourage the progressive development of skills.

Individual study or project work may be an assessment feature of both A and AS syllabuses, and where appropriate, it may be a compulsory requirement of such syllabuses.

Most of the biology syllabuses that have been developed recently contain an investigative module. Some examination boards have a compulsory or an optional module with respect to projects. Such a project can be used to assess a multitude of skills that are extremely useful in the working situation, and this trend should be encouraged.

Increasingly tertiary courses require students to carry out project work.

I have used the term teacher throughout, meaning not only a teacher of the sixth form in a school but also a lecturer in a college or university.

This third volume, *Investigating*, brings together many of the skills that can be developed by using the first two volumes in the series. One cannot really begin an investigation cold – certain skills have to be acquired prior to the planning stage. Planning cannot take place in a vacuum – it must be based not only on knowledge but also on the skills that can be brought to bear on the situation.

Investigating describes the processes that one has to go through when carrying out a project. It includes strategies on the selection of a topic, background reading, generating hypotheses, designing experiments, suitable and appropriate techniques, carrying out preliminary work and the full-scale investigation, and finally writing up the report. *Investigating* leads the student carefully through the process, giving concrete examples for clarification.

Such a book is invaluable in the planning and execution of a project. Since individual projects are one-offs and therefore unique in their own way, it is impossible to foresee the outcomes. There is a great element of uncertainty which can cause difficulties, but there is however a methodology which can be followed, since there is a general pattern to all investigations. So why make it harder than it needs to be?

The project is often the only *real* science that students experience – the process by which scientific knowledge is obtained. This book enables students to begin to think like biologists and to experience what real research work is like, or at least to get a feel for the scientific method of enquiry.

When the project is complete your students will have a most useful and important resource, properly written up and produced on a wordprocessor.

To the student

Increasingly you will be required to develop those skills that will be useful to you not only in your examinations but also in later life. The jobs of the future will require you to apply knowledge, some of which is known at present but much of which is not yet known. You will be required to solve problems and to come up with new ideas.

Perhaps you have to carry out a project as a requirement of your course, or you are thinking about the possibility of doing one if it is optional. Always take that option since you will learn to develop skills that will be extremely useful to you in all sorts of situations.

Carrying out an appropriate investigation means that you can gain marks prior to the examination. It will also help you to answer questions in the examination which deal with investigative work.

Investigative work always seems to create problems because of uncertainty – since a particular investigation is open-ended no-one knows what the outcomes will be before the work is started, so you will be working somewhat in the dark. This can be unsettling and make you feel insecure. It is often difficult to decide on a suitable topic; the topic chosen is usually far too complicated, and above all it can be very difficult to actually get started.

On the other hand it can be extremely exciting to be working on something that is uniquely yours – to find out something that no-one has ever found out before – as in *Star Trek* 'to boldly go where no man has gone before'. When you carry out a project you will probably know more about that particular topic than anyone else, at least those in your institution. Such work will make you think, you will have to be well organised, and above all persistent in the face of difficulties – you will have to face problems head on, and overcome them. But the rewards are worth it.

This book will help you through the processes of carrying out an investigation in biology or human biology. Don't forget to consult your teacher when you are selecting a topic to investigate, when you have your investigation planned, and at any other time that you feel is necessary. Always discuss your work with your fellow students.

All the best

JWG   1995

Acknowledgements

To the following from the School of Biology and Biochemistry at Queen's University: Dr Max Lewis and Dr Paul Clifford for reading the manuscript and offering useful suggestions; Dr Pete Laming for his constructive ideas.

To Denmour Boyd, for his help in supplying ideas, particularly in ecology.

To the following from the School of Education at Queen's University: Dr Tony Gallagher for his help with questionnaire design, and Earl Robinson for explaining why a Latin Square is so called.

To Alastair Edwards of the Northern Ireland Education Support Unit for all his help.

To Roger Lock from the School of Education, Birmingham University.

To all my former students from Cambridge House Girls' and Boys' Grammar Schools who undertook project work, and in particular those who supplied examples of their projects.

To my co-travellers Des O'Rawe and Liam McAleese whose discussions over coffee were so illuminating.

To my wife Betty for her patience and understanding.

To my editor Sarah Ware for her patience and good sense.

Finally I would like to thank all those at Stanley Thornes (Publishers) Ltd for their help – in particular Adrian Wheaton and Malcolm Tomlin who had the problem of getting it all together.

The publishers are grateful to the following for permission to reproduce copyright material:
Association for Science Education: adapted extracts from *School Science Review*, pp. 26, 75.
British Library: manuscript, p. 4.
David Scharf/Science Photo Library: photograph p. 28.
Dr Jeremy Burgess/Science Photo Library: photograph p. 83.
Empics/Witters: photograph, p. 71 (upper).
Journal of Membrane Biology: extract, p. 63.
JW Spear & Sons PLC: the board game Scrabble® is featured on pp. 9–13. Scrabble® is a registered trademark. Reproduced by kind permission of JW Spear & Sons PLC.
London Scientific Films/OSF: photograph, p. 28.
Martyn F Chillmaid: photographs, pp. 9, 10, 40, 44, 60, 71 (lower), 76, 78.
Mary Evans Picture Library: portrait, p. 61.
Science Footage: video stills, p. 98.
All other photographs are by the author.

The publishers have made every effort to contact copyright holders and apologise if any have been overlooked.

1 Introduction

1.1 WHAT IS SCIENCE?

The starting point of science is curiosity – we can describe scientists as very curious people! They simply want to know why things are the ways they are. Curiosity is something that we normally associate with young children. They are always asking – What is that? How does that work? What is that for? and so on. For some reason or other we tend to lose this questioning attitude as we grow older. Is it just part of maturing or does our education play a part by not encouraging and developing this most important attitude?

In many ways being a scientist means that we have to retain the child-like qualities of curiosity and questioning into adult life – a sort of mental neoteny (a biological term that is used to describe the retention of larval features in the adult form). This quality of curiosity is I believe normally just submerged and simply needs encouragement and a bit of practice to get it brought to the surface. We all have this ability, but it tends to lie dormant. We need to continue to ask questions, let alone try to find the answers to them.

Because of their nature, all investigations will be personal to the person concerned, and biology covers a multitude of areas. There are, however, general factors in common with all investigations, no matter how involved they are, or what topic they cover.

This diagram of the **science cycle** summarises the process of investigating.

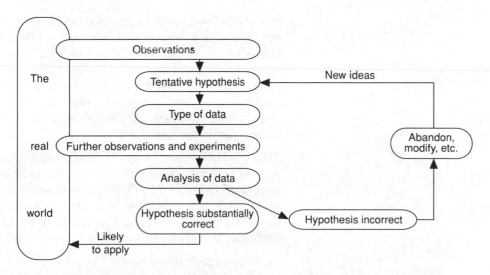

Science is about discovering. It involves both knowledge and the process by which that knowledge is obtained. This is the strength of science – it is a cycle involving a **positive feedback** mechanism. You will probably meet such feedback systems in biology. As the process produces more knowledge, then the knowledge in turn affects the process, which in turn produces more knowledge.

This book, in fact the series *Skills in Advanced Biology*, is not in the main concerned with the knowledge of science but with the processes. Maybe it could be described as knowledge of the process.

Scientists inquire into the natural world, trying to make sense of it. They work in industry, in universities and in research establishments. Some probably teach and do some administration but most of them carry out research, write scientific papers and read research papers at conferences. To do this they receive research grants – they can have expensive equipment, good technical backup and good library facilities. They will also be in close communication with others not only in this country but throughout the world – using electronic mail and the Internet has greatly speeded up this communication.

Scientists want to push back the frontiers of knowledge, discovering little by little how the universe operates. Biologists are often motivated by human suffering, trying to alleviate it where possible. The work that they are doing is often unique since one biologist might be the only person working in that particular area. Above all, true scientists are honest – they abhor anyone who cheats, either by falsifying data or by stealing someone else's work. There are actually various ways in which 'cheating' can occur. Irregularities in the data can be removed to make them more acceptable and precise; only those results that fit the theory can be retained, the others disregarded; and invented data can be reported. The most common accusation is that of 'plagiarism' where ideas or writings of others are presented as one's own. Due acknowledgement of others' work should always be given.

Scientists think roughly in a particular way although the work that they are doing can be very unpredictable and they might have to change direction when it is required. They operate from a base of knowledge and they possess a range of particular skills, both mental and manual. They must be adaptable and use their scientific know-how which has been developed over the years, and apply it to new situations. They must be prepared to change their minds and try something different; in other words they must have a particular set of attitudes.

This scientific know-how only comes from actually doing science. In many ways it is similar to the abilities that good games players, chess masters, expert musicians and gifted teachers acquire. By carrying out successful investigations they become better at them. Often they are not aware of what they are actually doing, finding it difficult to analyse, describe and explain their mental processes and actions.

So, to be able to do science we need specialised knowledge, special skills, special attitudes and flair. The only effective way therefore to learn to do science is by doing science alongside someone who is skilled and experienced and so can provide on-the-job criticism and advice. That is why someone who is setting out on a career as a researcher is always supported by a supervisor.

1.2 SCHOOL SCIENCE

School science is in the main very different from what scientists actually do. You will have only a limited knowledge of biology by the time you enter the sixth form or introductory tertiary courses, and only limited skills required for investigating. Much of your time will now be spent acquiring further biological knowledge and developing certain skills – so that you will do well in your exams.

GCSE science and biology has recognised the importance of investigative skills, albeit in a simplified form. Following on from these developments many changes have taken place in A-level syllabuses, GNVQ and other courses, which place more and more emphasis on the development of such skills. You will have brought with you from GCSE certain skills and attitudes that will help you with this type of work. You now have the opportunity to develop these skills further and to participate in 'real' science.

1.3 TYPES OF INVESTIGATIONS

There are many different levels of investigating in biology that are employed in sixth-form and equivalent courses, introductory third-level courses, etc.

What is actually meant by an investigation? Roger Lock, in an article in the *School Science Review* (March 1990 – see if you can find it!), suggests that an investigation is often seen as 'an experimental study that requires first-hand student participation and leads towards providing evidence that permits a question, posed at the outset, to be answered'. He goes on to suggest that this general statement allows considerable variation and gives a number of possibilities; the diagram below is a simplified version of his model.

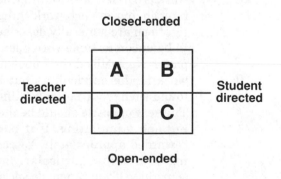

1.3.1 'Recipe' experiments

In the diagram above, A represents a typical experiment carried out in many types of courses. Such experiments are of the 'recipe' type where you follow a set of instructions on a worksheet (the recipe) and hope that the results (the cake) turn out as expected. Students (and teachers) feel secure with well-structured worksheets – you know exactly what you should do, in the order that you should do it. Not only that, you probably know, or can guess, the answer before you carry out the experiment since it is implied in the title and the theory will probably have been discussed beforehand. This type of experiment confirms what is already known. As an example of this type of experiment, a worksheet could be titled 'To show that amylase breaks down starch'. Experiments like this only show that you can follow instructions (called protocols in research), but they can help you to develop particular techniques like manipulating apparatus, making up solutions, recording and analysing results, etc.

The worksheet title might appear to be more open-ended, for example 'To find the effect of amylase on starch' and you might or might not know before you carry out the experiment what the amylase does to the starch. This is nevertheless still 'recipe' science since you would simply be following instructions decided upon by your teacher.

1.3.2 Guided discovery

Returning to the diagram on page 3, in the situation at B your teacher asks a question which you then try to answer by an experiment or series of experiments. For example you might be asked 'What is the effect of amylase on starch?' You have to plan and carry out experiments to answer this question. You will use the knowledge and skills acquired from earlier theory and practical work to help you. From this type of work you develop planning skills and you will obtain data that you will have to analyse. Generally however your teacher will know the results that should be obtained and there still tend to be 'right' answers. Such situations are useful in teaching you how to hypothesise and design experiments but as in recipe experiments, the situation is contrived.

1.3.3 Open-ended investigations

This is the situation at C. Open-ended investigations differ from recipe experiments and guided discovery by the fact that neither the student nor the teacher knows what the results or outcomes are going to be before the work is carried out. Your teacher might have some idea about what might happen, but in such work things rarely turn out as expected. Such investigations are generally described as projects. Students and teachers tend to be uncomfortable with open-ended work. Many educationalists in the past have realised the importance of including open-ended investigatory work in the curriculum, but it has often floundered because students found such work not only difficult, but stressful and often unrewarding. The very opposite should be the case – you should find it exciting, rewarding and stimulating. If it is considered important, then it should be rewarded appropriately. You can be given the opportunity of investigating an area that particularly interests you, or your teacher could suggest something if you cannot decide on a topic of your own. If your teacher assists or directs you along particular lines then we move more to position D in the diagram.

Some scientific work at school, at least towards the end of the secondary phase and certainly in the introductory phase of tertiary education, should be open-ended. This is 'real' science. For such work to be worthwhile however, it is necessary for the investigator to have not only a sound background knowledge of biology but also a basic level of competence in the skills of manipulating apparatus, analysing data, etc. Volumes 1 and 2 in this series were concerned with the development of such skills. As you acquire the knowledge and develop the necessary skills during the earlier part of your course you will become more confident in tackling the unknown, but you must have the tools to do the job. Actually much of 'doing' science is 'inside the head' – it is the matter of thinking scientifically that is important. It is therefore only during the latter part of your course that you will acquired the necessary knowledge and skills to tackle an open-ended investigation.

There are plenty of books dealing with the knowledge of biology and the recipe type of experimenting. This volume is concerned mainly with the open-ended type of investigating and should dispel some of the myths and difficulties of engaging in such work.

Syllabuses and curricula increasingly require you to carry out some sort of investigation. Perhaps all that is required is a short investigation where the problem is given to you by your teacher and the practical work need not be more than for an open-ended laboratory experiment, but the results or data should be more complete, and the report should be more detailed. On the other hand you might have to carry out a much longer project where you have to think up the topic yourself, albeit in discussion with your teacher, plan the investigation which could involve a number of experiments, and carry it out yourself.

What do we therefore mean by a biological investigation or project? In general it

1. is an investigation involving inquiry into some aspect of biology;
2. is carried out by an individual student;
3. requires more time than is normally available during one practical session;
4. involves formulating hypotheses, testing by experiments or surveys, obtaining quantitative results, and analysis of those results;
5. involves writing up a report in a scientific style.

It is better if it is your own individual work, but you could work with others in a group if you are looking at different aspects of the same topic. The report should however always be your own work. You will be assessed on your work and particularly on your report.

Remember that your investigation need not be specifically experimental in the sense of setting up an artificial situation to test a hypothesis. Investigations can involve careful observation, description and analysis, by carrying out surveys in the field or of people.

The main thing is that your teacher will act as an adviser, consultant and mentor, giving you the opportunity to make your own decisions, but guiding and helping you to proceed along fruitful lines when required.

1.4 IMPORTANCE OF INVESTIGATIVE WORK

Open-ended investigating is an essential part of the education and training of biologists since it gives first-hand experience of some of the procedures and methods of original research – in a simpler, but significant way. It places emphasis on a sound scientific approach involving a range of various activities like careful reading of the literature, discussion with colleagues, good design, careful planning and organisation of the practical work, sound laboratory practice, critical analysis and interpretation of results, to appropriate presentation of the work in a report.

When you are working on a particular topic you will in all possibility know more about it than anyone else, at least within your institution. Your project will in all likelihood therefore be unique, because you are unique! Creativity implies the ideas coming out of someone's head – think of poetry, music, art, etc. The same should happen in science. Such work can give you not only a real 'kick' but also a sense of what it is like to carry out research. Your curiosity should be aroused if you feel that what you have been doing is exciting and worthwhile. You will learn that some questions and problems do not have a definitive right answer – some solutions are tentative and need to be refined, requiring further information or needing further inquiry – some might even be compromises. You could even be disappointed that at the end of your project, because of time constraints, you are unable to continue the work. Do not forget that pure research, arising out of nothing more than sheer curiosity, can be just as important as applied research where a distinct problem needs to be solved. We never really know what is going to be important and what is not. We cannot look into the future and predict, much as we would like to.

The skills that you develop as a result of a proper investigation are invaluable not only as a preparation for higher education, but also for whatever work you will be involved in eventually.

Remember that if you are going to apply for a place in higher education, interviews usually take place during the spring of your last year. It is worth taking your project along with you, not only to let your interviewers see what you are capable of, but it can also be a good starting point for discussion.

More and more employers are looking for those skills which can only be developed through open-ended investigatory work – ability to search databases and the literature, to solve problems, to come up with ideas, to test hypotheses, to design experiments, to analyse data, to write and present reports, etc. As well as these skills, you will have learnt (hopefully) how to overcome difficulties, how to use your initiative, creativity, perseverance, planning, and above all common (maybe we should call it uncommon) sense. Nothing can compare with investigative work as a means of self-development and preparation for the future.

In summary, in order to carry out constructive open-ended investigations you will need to have

1. a sound but broad knowledge of biology;
2. a sound background knowledge of the specific topic you are considering;
3. a clear understanding of how to set about a scientific investigation;
4. the ability to perform certain operations safely and successfully;
5. a certain amount of flair in carrying out the work in an organised and skilful way;
6. confidence, commitment and determination.

1.5 DIFFICULTIES OF INVESTIGATIVE WORK

Investigative or project work always seems to cause problems. We have already come across some of the reasons why students and teachers alike have difficulties with such work. What are the other reasons? Teachers and students seem to be more confident with clearly defined situations – students usually say to themselves 'If I learn this topic well and it turns up in an examination, then I will be able to answer it properly and I will obtain good marks and thus pass my examination!' This is important, but such situations do not help you to acquire those skills and attitudes that are essential for personal development and the ability to work well and effectively. And remember that investigative work is now part of the assessment!

The main problems arise from the fact that most investigative work takes place in the head. The actual experimental or observational process is only attempting to confirm or otherwise what we had been imagining or visualising.

From many years of experience with such work I have found that attention needs to be focused on the following four key areas:

1. choosing a topic
2. proper and adequate design
3. keeping the investigation within bounds
4. getting down to the work.

These areas will be dealt with in detail in Chapter 5 – Planning Investigations.

2 Scientific Method and Investigating

2.1 IS THERE A SCIENTIFIC METHOD?

What is called the **scientific method** is usually a rather simplified account of what goes on during the process of making scientific discoveries or of solving scientific problems. There is of course pure and applied scientific research – pure research results from simply wanting to know, while applied research deals with specific problems and how to solve them. The scientific method is a way of deciding what is true from what is untrue (or at least less true). It is however more straightforward to show that something is untrue – a hypothesis can by one fact be shown to be false, or at least require to be modified.

Basically the process is simple and straightforward – from the observation of facts, a hypothesis (tentative idea or assumption) is suggested; this hypothesis is then tested by experiment and/or the accumulation of more facts relevant to the situation; this process is continued so that an understanding of the topic under investigation is built up. Nothing should appeal to our common sense more than this!

The label 'scientific' method implies that its use is limited to scientists; in fact it is available to everyone and is gradually being used more and more in many walks of life. To know about this method is therefore useful in many work situations and the skills learnt are transferable.

The scientific method essentially involves the following steps:

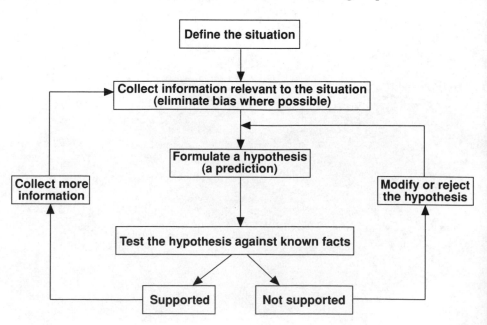

The scientific method brings together fact and idea (**observation** and **hypothesis**). The important thing to notice is that the process is cyclical, always testing hypotheses and thus rejecting, refining or coming up with new hypotheses as further information becomes available. Science is on-going, always building on what has gone before. Knowledge and skills improve as time passes.

Scientists must therefore always be prepared to change their minds if necessary – they don't make sweeping assertions, but speak with caution and humility. This is the great strength of science, not a weakness. This is not always appreciated or understood by others, especially non-scientists and media people. This tentative approach can cause confusion and produce an attitude that scientists don't know what they are talking about. Scientists need to put their case more strongly – the scientific method is strong and can highlight the weaknesses of other ways of operating. Increasingly the scientific method is being used in other areas of human endeavour.

2.2 A MODEL OF THE SCIENTIFIC METHOD

Let us look at an example of the mental processes that operate when thinking scientifically. Scientists often use models which enable them to visualise the situation better. Take for example the board game Scrabble®. We can use this game as a model of scientific thinking.

The situation

To achieve the highest score by using the letter tiles to form interlocking words on the board.

Facts relevant to the situation

The tiles with letters and numbers
Each letter has a different value marked on it and there are different numbers of letters per set as shown below.

Letter	A	B	C	D	E	F	G	H	I	J	K	L	M	N	O	P	Q	R	S	T	U	V	W	X	Y	Z	◯
Points value	1	3	3	2	1	4	2	4	1	8	5	1	3	1	1	3	10	1	1	1	1	4	4	8	4	10	Blank
Number in set	9	2	2	4	12	2	3	2	9	1	1	4	2	6	8	2	1	6	4	6	4	2	2	1	2	1	2

1 Can you find any relationship between the letters and the points values?

The board

This consists of a large number of squares some of which are labelled DOUBLE LETTER SCORE (DL), TRIPLE LETTER SCORE (TL), DOUBLE WORD SCORE (DW) and TRIPLE WORD SCORE (TW). If a tile is placed on a square labelled DOUBLE LETTER SCORE, then the value of that letter is doubled. If a letter of a word falls in the DOUBLE WORD SCORE square then the total value of that word is doubled.

The diagram below shows part of the board, with the starting point at ★.

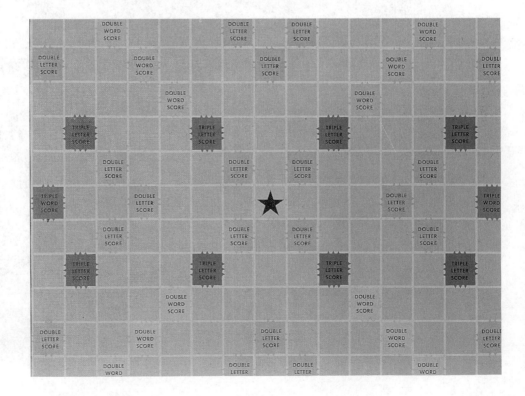

The rules

These are given in the rule book, but the best way to learn the rules is to 'have a go'. Let us assume that the order of play has been decided – you go first (that is good since the first square is a DOUBLE WORD SCORE). You draw seven tiles from the bag and place them on your rack. They are as follows:

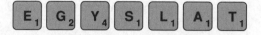

You look at them, move them around, thinking of a word that you can make from them. An interactive process of observing and thinking takes place, using your memory store of words. By juggling the letters around you might by accident hit on a word or on a sequence of letters that give you a clue. You put the S and the Y over at the right-hand side of the rack since they often come at the end of words.

Then an idea (Hypothesis 1) comes to you – ATE.

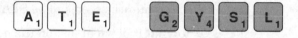

You now evaluate this idea by mentally working out the score. It is not very good: $3[1\times3] \times 2[\text{DW}] = $ **6**.

You now think again. Could I make it a four-letter word? It comes to you – a better idea (Hypothesis 2) – add the L to ATE to give

This has a better score: $4[1\times4] \times 2[\text{DW}] = $ **8**.

However, you are not very happy with this since each of the letters has a value of only 1 and you have higher value letters left. You look at the tiles again and think – it comes to you – change the L for a G, so your next idea (Hypothesis 3) is

The score is still improving: $5 \times 2 = $ **10**.

You now notice that if it was a five-letter word then the last letter would have a double score (see board). You suddenly remember about plurals and you have an S! Your next idea (Hypothesis 4) is therefore

The score is still rising: $7[2+1+1+ 1+ 2] \times 2 = $ **14**.

Doing better. But you think – it is a pity that the last letter (S) has a value of only 1. You go back to the beginning again, shuffling all the letters around and thinking about the letters in new arrangements. You come up with a different idea (Hypothesis 5) – SLATE.

This has a score of 6[1+1+1+1+2] × 2 = **12**, which is less than your previous idea – no good. Pity that all the letters in SLATE have a value of 1 only. You look at the high value Y(4) and suddenly you think that it might go at the end instead of the E to give SLATY (Hypothesis 6).

This would give a score of 12[1+1+1+1+8] × 2 = **24**. Very good – by far the best.

You wonder however if there is such a word, and if so, is it spelt slaty or slatey? You think there could be such a word, probably meaning slate-like as in colour, for example. You decide to take a chance – the score is high even though it might be challenged. Your best solution under the circumstances seems to be SLATY.

You put it down at last on the board; it is challenged by your partner; the dictionary is produced and it is declared a valid word. So far so good.

Thinking scientifically

The processes whereby you arrived at SLATY all went on in your head, but they were assisted by careful observation. You were in effect testing a series of hypotheses. This is exactly what goes on during the process of scientific investigation. Often looking at things in a different way, what is sometimes called **lateral thinking** (a term coined by Edward de Bono), can help in the creation of worthwhile hypotheses. You might even come up with something much better than SLATY – have a go!

Let us continue the game. Your opponent places the word PLOT on the board – a short word with a score of 6 but the P lies on a DOUBLE WORD SCORE so it is worth **12** points.

			P	
			L	
			O	
S	L	A	T	Y

Among the five new tiles that have replaced the ones you put on the board there is an S. You can quite easily add this to PLOT and get a score of 7.

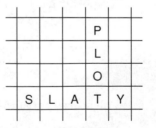

Your opponent comes up with a good one, since she had an X, worth 8 points – FLUX

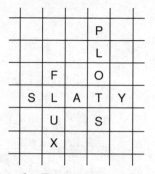

This was a good score since the F (4 points) and U (1 point) were on DOUBLE LETTER SCORES so the score is 8+1+2+8 = **19**.

And so the game goes on – new situations arising, but these have similarities to the previous situations. There are ground-rules which we can follow. Each situation is however unique, since each time we draw tiles from the bag, the combinations are different. We have to adapt to such new situations, continually refining and improving our knowledge and understanding of the situation.

Most importantly you improve at the game by actually playing it – this goes for all games. By playing Scrabble® you improve your knowledge and your skills – the more that you play the better you are able to play. This is known as positive feedback and is the reason why you will develop a flair for the game after playing it for some time. Science is no different – only by actually investigating will you get better at it!

Science can be hindered from moving forward by the perceived dogma existing at any particular time. New ideas (paradigms) have difficulty surviving in such an environment. As the tortoise said 'In order to move forward I have to stick my neck out'. Only when the work is repeated by others and verified does it gradually become absorbed into the main body of scientific knowledge. Scientists regularly make unique contributions early on in their careers, before they become too conditioned by established practice.

2.3 CREATIVITY IN SCIENCE

Scientific originality is often thought to reside in making new hypotheses – in either putting together existing knowledge and ideas in unusual combinations or coming up with new ideas. Some people are good at asking such new questions, but this is only part of the equation – good experiments must be designed and carried out in order to test the hypotheses.

Such work requires a high level of creativity. Creativity is usually associated with the arts – music, drama and writing for example – but it plays a crucial and central role in science.

Imagine a poet writing a poem, or a composer composing a symphony, or an artist painting a picture. We realise how good they are at such things only when we try to attempt them ourselves. Why are we so poor at them?

Well, to start with, we lack the necessary knowledge and skills. Before starting to compose the composer must possess basic knowledge and skills, for example, knowing all about the various musical instruments – their sounds, their range, what players can and cannot do, etc. Knowledge of musical theory is important. The composer then has an idea for the symphony, or concerto or whatever, and using knowledge and skills converts this idea into reality. The tune is put down as staff notation. The first attempts are usually rough, and they require more and more correction and refinement until the end result is as near as possible to the idea that the composer had thought of at the start.

Poets or writers of any sort obviously have ideas in their heads before putting them down on paper – they conform to the conventions of grammar and normal usuage, spelling, etc. They must have these skills – also the skill of using words so that the reader understands what the writer is getting at. At present I am using words to try and create images in your heads. What I am writing is as near as possible as I can get to what is going on in my head. This is not always as easy as you might think!

Similar situations often occur in science. When Watson and Crick were attempting to work out the structure of the DNA molecule they developed a knowledge base, mainly from the work of others, which they brought to bear on the problem. They developed hypotheses regarding the structure of DNA, and, using their knowledge and skills, tried them out by building models. They gradually modified these until they arrived at a structure which satisifed all the criteria.

Science has so much in common with other areas of human endeavour. Why then do many people have difficulty relating to science as a creative human activity which has brought us immense benefits and reduced massively human suffering?

2.4 SERENDIPITY IN SCIENCE

Chance in science is far more important than generally realised. Although great steps forward can be made by an observation exhibiting an effect which was not intended – much of science moves forward by the addition of many small chance effects – once experiments are carried out all sorts of effects can come into play, and they cannot be foreseen. Even after the event it is often difficult to piece together which parts were important and which were unimportant.

Great scientists of the past understood the importance of change. Francis Bacon, considered by most as the father of science, in his *Novum Organum* (1620) stated: 'Hence all the most Noble Discoveries have (if you observe) come to light, not by any gradual improvement and Extension of the arts, but merely by Chance' . . . and Pasteur has written that 'Chance favours the prepared mind'.

The usual word for chance in science is **serendipity**. This can be described as something unusual or extraordinary that has not been searched for, but has been detected by either plain curiosity, meticulous observation, sagacity (foresight; ability to make good judgements) or lateral thinking. It often occurs as a result of a 'mistake' in the experimental setup.

The following two examples are typical of what can happen.

Millardet's 'Bordeaux mixture'

During the 1880s the vineyards of France were being decimated by the downy mildew fungus (*Plasmopara viticola*). The Professor of Botany at Bordeaux, Pierre Marie Alexis Millardet worked out the life cycle of the fungus and determined to stop this fungus from destroying the French wine industry.

In 1882 Millardet visited one of the vineyards in southwest France – the following is an account of what happened. This extract is taken from *Advance of the Fungi* by E. C. Large (Jonathan Cape, 1940).

> Towards the end of October, in the year 1882, Professor Millardet was strolling through one of the vineyards of Saint-Julien in Médoc. There had been much Mildew in the locality that year, and he was surprised to notice that the vines beside the path were still in leaf, while elsewhere they were bare. He paused to examine these leaves which had escaped the common fate, and he found traces on them of a bluish-white deposit, as though they had received some chemical treatment. This was interesting, and he made inquiries about it of Mr. Ernest David, who was the manager of the vineyards at the Château Beaucaillon. He learned that it was a custom of the vinegrowers of Médoc to bespatter the vines beside the paths with a conspicuous and poisonous-looking substance, to discourage the passers-by from pilfering the grapes. For this they used either verdigris or a mixture of copper sulphate and lime. Mr. David had never given the matter a thought, but now that the Professor mentioned it, those vines beside the paths, for all that they were so disfigured, did appear greener and more healthy than the rest.

So Millardet noticed, but the vineyard manager Monsieur David hadn't, that the vines beside the paths that had been sprinkled with the chemical to discourage passers-by from pilfering the grapes were not affected by the mildew, whereas those vines further back that hadn't been treated were affected by the mildew. Millardet had perceived something that no-one had seen, even those who were working in the vineyard daily! Millardet was of course searching frantically for a remedy to rid the vines of the mildew since the whole economy, let alone the way of life, of France was at stake. He was therefore alert to anything that might help him.

Millardet went on to test his hypothesis that copper salts would kill the fungus, and he eventually came up with Bordeaux mixture, the first fungicide to be used on a large scale.

Fertility from the freezer

This example is an adaptation from *The Silent Revolution* by Quentin Seddon (BBC Books, 1989) and concerns the role of a mistake which resulted in the important discovery of the freezing of animal cells so that they remain viable for lengthy periods of time. The courtroom dramas at present which concern fertility drugs, test-tube babies, embryo transplants and surrogate mothers all started with efforts to improve traditional breeding methods on the farm. Artificial insemination was carried out for many years using live semen but there were problems of timing and transport. If sperm, ova and even embryos could be frozen and retain their viability then the science and practice of reproduction would be revolutionised.

It all started in 1948 in one of the laboratories at the National Institute for Medical Research. For many years there had been reports that semen could survive freezing to very low temperatures, and that it would be viable when thawed out. If such reports were true, then sperm could be preserved for long periods of time and artificial insemination would become a more flexible and powerful system for breeding. Chris Polge tried the recommended technique on fowl sperm – mixing it with the sugar fructose laevulose and freezing it rapidly to the temperature of solid carbon dioxide. The semen died. He tried again and again but always the semen died. He continued to persist but after months of trying and getting nowhere he eventually gave up.

The opportunity to renew the work came about and Polge thought he would have another go. He sent for the remains of his fructose laevulose solution. He proceeded as before but this time when the sperm cells were thawed out they swam about merrily, none the worse for their period of hibernation. Why did the technique work this time when it didn't work before?

The stock of sugar solution was running out so new solutions were made up. When these were tried no sperm cells survived. Chris Polge did however have a small amount of the successful sugar solution left in its original bottle. Maybe the sugar had somehow been changed, perhaps by contamination with a mould. When it was analysed however, it was found that instead of sugar, all that was present was glycerol, water and the protein albumen – it was in fact 'Meyer's albumen' – used by histologists when coating glass slides.

It was then discovered that, standing next to the bottle with the fructose laevulose solution on a shelf above the work-bench, there was a bottle containing Meyer's albumen. It seems that the laboratory technician who was preparing the fructose solution for freezing made a mistake and used the Meyer's albumen instead. Polge went on to try glycerol and found that fowl semen could be preserved indefinitely by freezing in it.

From this chance breakthrough with fowl semen, the whole artificial insemination programme in cattle took off. Time and thus distance were unimportant. You could obtain semen from the best bulls, freeze it in liquid nitrogen, and use it to fertilise cows thousands of miles away, or even years after the bulls were dead.

Once the idea of using glycerol had worked with semen, it was eventually used with eggs and early embryos. From that simple error of the bottles a whole industry has grown up.

Most really new discoveries are made by chance in experiments designed for other purposes. First hypotheses are more often wrong than correct.

When we get results that we don't expect we can check by replicating (repeating exactly). If the results reoccur then they can lead to modified or even new hypotheses.

2.5 SCIENTIFIC DISCOVERIES

So many events impinge on scientific discoveries that it is extremely difficult to have any foresight of what will happen – the discovery of penicillin is a case in point, as illustrated on pages 18–19. It is given in some detail just to show how many factors played a part in what is often cited as a simple example of a chance discovery in science. The whole process in developing penicillin as an effective antibiotic was a complex one, involving many individuals together with a large number of events coming together that could not have been predicted.

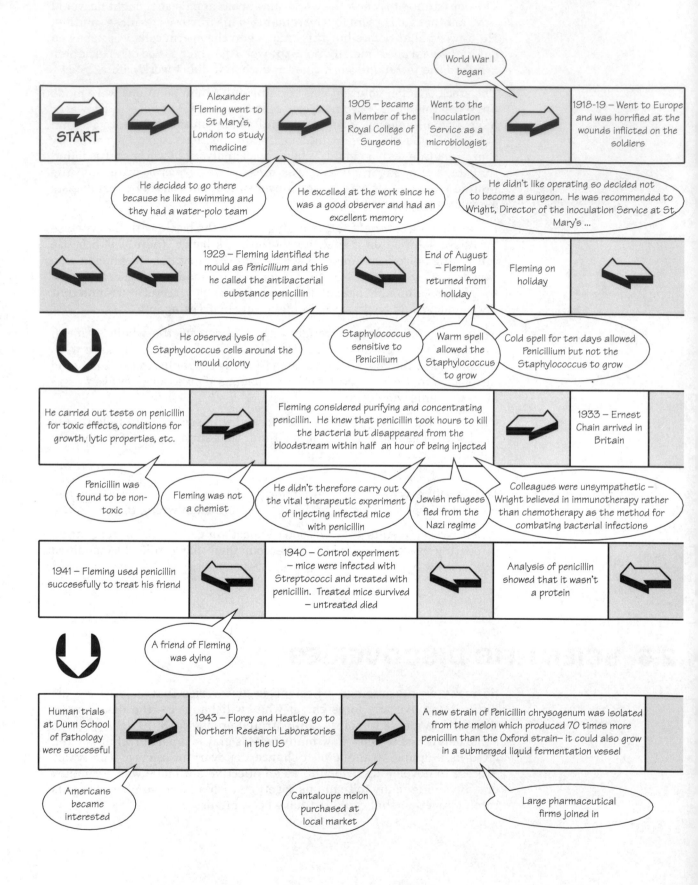

START

Alexander Fleming went to St Mary's, London to study medicine

1905 – became a Member of the Royal College of Surgeons

Went to the Inoculation Service as a microbiologist

World War I began

1918-19 – Went to Europe and was horrified at the wounds inflicted on the soldiers

He decided to go there because he liked swimming and they had a water-polo team

He excelled at the work since he was a good observer and had an excellent memory

He didn't like operating so decided not to become a surgeon. He was recommended to Wright, Director of the inoculation Service at St Mary's ...

1929 – Fleming identified the mould as *Penicillium* and this he called the antibacterial substance penicillin

End of August – Fleming returned from holiday

Fleming on holiday

He observed lysis of Staphylococcus cells around the mould colony

Staphylococcus sensitive to Penicillium

Warm spell allowed the Staphylococcus to grow

Cold spell for ten days allowed Penicillium but not the Staphylococcus to grow

He carried out tests on penicillin for toxic effects, conditions for growth, lytic properties, etc.

Fleming considered purifying and concentrating penicillin. He knew that penicillin took hours to kill the bacteria but disappeared from the bloodstream within half an hour of being injected

1933 – Ernest Chain arrived in Britain

Penicillin was found to be non-toxic

Fleming was not a chemist

He didn't therefore carry out the vital therapeutic experiment of injecting infected mice with penicillin

Jewish refugees fled from the Nazi regime

Colleagues were unsympathetic – Wright believed in immunotherapy rather than chemotherapy as the method for combating bacterial infections

1941 – Fleming used penicillin successfully to treat his friend

1940 – Control experiment – mice were infected with Streptococci and treated with penicillin. Treated mice survived – untreated died

Analysis of penicillin showed that it wasn't a protein

A friend of Fleming was dying

Human trials at Dunn School of Pathology were successful

1943 – Florey and Heatley go to Northern Research Laboratories in the US

A new strain of Penicillin chrysogenum was isolated from the melon which produced 70 times more penicillin than the Oxford strain– it could also grow in a submerged liquid fermentation vessel

Americans became interested

Cantaloupe melon purchased at local market

Large pharmaceutical firms joined in

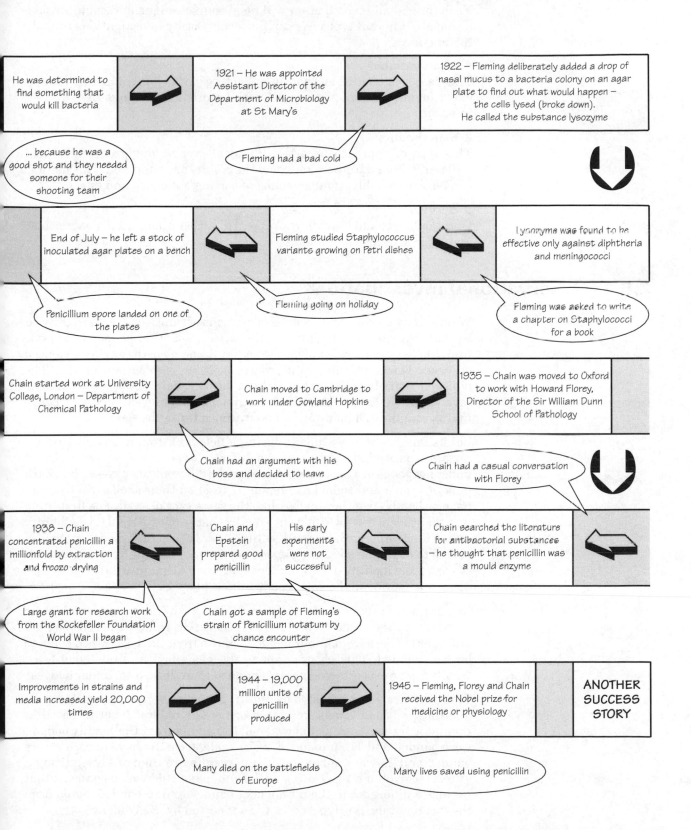

2.6 TYPES OF INVESTIGATIONS

Each individual investigation will be of course unique and could involve a range of different types. We can however classify investigations roughly by function.

1 Observational

This is a systematic method of collecting data. We could call it non-experimental biology. We quantify characteristics of things that we find in nature.

2 Experimental

This type of approach uses two identical groups; one group is treated differently from the other group and the results are compared. This method can be a reasonably reliable means of sorting out cause and effect.

3 Surveys

Questionnaires and interviews are used to gather information about people and their attitudes or opinions.

2.6.1 Observational investigations

We start any investigation with observations of things or events in the real world. They can be stimulated by the writings of other biologists or arise from the keen perception of the observer. Remember that an experienced observer perceives things differently from an inexperienced one. The biologist usually makes observations 'in the field' and the organisms involved are disturbed as little as possible. Such observations can involve taking complicated monitoring apparatus out into the field.

Let us imagine that a student during a fieldwork course observes that a certain type of snail seems to have a different appearance if they are found under hedges or in a beechwood. They can be different colours – yellow, dark pink or brown and some have bands (1 to 5) on their shells while others have no bands – yet they all look like the same type of snail. The first thing that the student does is to find out exactly what species of snail it is. A library search for an appropriate identification guide soon establishes that they all belong to the same species – *Cepaea nemoralis*. It is vital that the species is accurately identified. Our student now knows that any differences that occur are not due to the snails being different species.

In what ways are the snails different? After examining a few snails from each habitat the student observes that the snails from the beechwood are different to those from under hedges – those from the beechwood seem to be less banded. This observation is the basis for the first hypothesis: 'Snails from the beechwood are less banded than those from under hedges'.

This hypothesis is then tested by counting the number of snails with bands and those without bands from each of the two habitats. Let us say that the numbers turn out as follows – of 150 snails from the beechwood, 40 were banded and 110 unbanded; of 70 snails from under hedges, 45 were banded and 25 were unbanded. These results are then analysed using a χ^2 test (see Volume 1 – *Dealing with Data*, page 105) which confirms that there is a difference in the numbers of banded and unbanded snails from the two habitats. So Hypothesis 1 is supported by the evidence.

However, closer examination of the data suggests that there were more banded snails found under the hedges than we would have expected by chance, and fewer banded ones from the beechwood, and conversely more unbanded ones from the beechwood and fewer from under the hedges. This information starts the student thinking again. Why should this be? Her general biological knowledge tells her that the banding pattern in some way helps the snails to survive better under hedges. If they are eaten by something then perhaps the banding pattern might have something to do with camouflage.

Discussions with colleagues and teachers come up with the suggestion that the snails might be eaten by birds. A library search produces a book that informs her that *Cepaea* is indeed a favourite food of song thrushes. During reading of this book she also learns that the thrush smashes open the shells on a suitable stone in its territory, appropriately called an anvil. If she could find anvils in each of the two habitats perhaps she could then find out if banding has anything to do with it. She thus comes up with her second hypothesis – that shell banding in the two habitats is the result of selective feeding by thrushes.

This process is continually repeated, the biologist getting better and better at asking questions which should result in arriving at better hypotheses which can then be tested.

She could, of course, try field experiments to find support or otherwise for her hypotheses. If her hypothesis was that the colour of the shell was related to the background as camouflage then she could remove snails from a diversified to a uniform habitat, from a mixed hedgerow to downland, and find out what happens to the population. She could place light coloured (yellow) *Cepaea* in woodlands and dark ones in grassland and find out what happens – would the thrushes eat more of them than the ones normally found there? This would be easy enough to find out. We shall be looking at elements of this process in more detail later. The student then goes on to try to explain what she has observed.

The process is cyclical – each testing of a hypothesis giving rise to further hypotheses, as shown in the flow diagram below.

The process of observational investigation

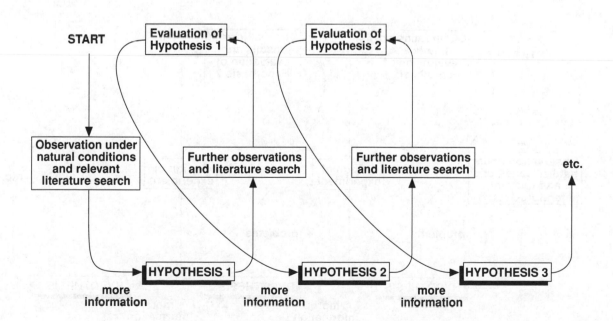

Examples of observational investigations would include – the distribution of particular organisms in particular habitats; morphological differences in the same organism in different habitats, for example, and trying to relate these to biotic and abiotic factors.

2.6.2 Experimental investigation

A student, during a biology lesson on leaf structure, was intrigued to find that the stomata open during the day and close at night. He decided that this would be a good topic to investigate.

Looking through his textbook and other books in the biology department he found that the stomatal aperture is controlled by the guard cells – if they are turgid the stoma is open, if flaccid it is closed. He wondered what caused these changes in the guard cells. Obviously the light must have something to do with it. His first hypothesis suggests itself.

He decided to vary the light and measure carefully the stomatal aperture at different light intensities. He also decided to use privet leaves since they were used in a recent practical on leaf peels when the class observed stomata under the microscope, and there was a privet hedge just outside the laboratory. He therefore had materials and the skills necessary to carry out the investigation.

He designed a simple setup whereby a bench lamp could be placed at varying distances from privet leaves – these were then painted with clear nail varnish and the peels examined under the microscope. From his knowledge of physics he knew about the inverse square law, but he measured the light intensity at varying distances using a light meter and from this information drew a conversion graph. When the lamp was very close to the leaf the temperature rose considerably, and since this could affect the stomatal aperture he had to devise a cooling device.

The process of experimental investigation

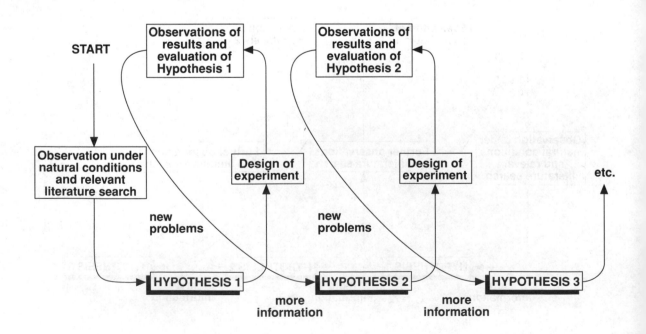

Once he had all his leaf peels carefully labelled with the light intensities he had to measure the stomatal apertures. To do this he used a graticule in the eyepiece of the microscope.

He finally drew a graph of stomatal aperture against light intensity.

Although he had found a relationship between the aperture and the light intensity he still wondered why the guard cells became turgid. He thought up a number of hypotheses which could be tested using a variety of experiments.

The process is similar to that for the observational investigation.

2.6.3 Surveys

A teacher was explaining to her human biology class that she had recently been to a biotechnology in-service course where she had heard about genetically modified tomatoes. The organiser of the course described how he had visited the commercial research company Zeneca and was one of the first to taste a puree made from the new tomatoes. Zeneca has since been granted a patent to sell tomato sauce and other products using these tomatoes.

As she listened one of the students wondered how people would react to such products once they reached the supermarket shelves. She thought that young people would be more likely to accept such innovations than older people and decided that this would be a suitable topic to investigate for the project that she had to carry out.

She arranged with her teacher to have a chat about it. The teacher was enthusiastic and suggested that a questionnaire would be a suitable method to find opinions on this matter.

The student went to the library to find out as much as she could about the new tomatoes and found a series of articles in the *New Scientist*. From these she discovered why scientists had developed the new tomato and how they had done it.

She decided to survey pupils in the school of a variety of ages and to get their parents to fill in questionnaires as well. What questions would she ask? She discussed this with her fellow students and her parents and came up with quite a few ideas. She tried them out with a small number of pupils of different ages and found that she had to explain things in more detail about the tomatoes before asking the questions.

She finally came up with a good selection of questions, checked them with her teacher who gave her a sample questionnaire which suggested to her ideas for layout. She then word-processed the questionnaire on one of the school computers and the laboratory technician ran her off 100 copies.

She obtained a random sample of 80 students of different ages and from these selected a sub-sample of 20 whose parents would be asked to complete the questionnaire.

Although she had to encourage some to complete the questionnaires she finally got them all back completed except one. She coded all the answers and put the numbers on a database on the school computer. Her analysis did indeed support her hypothesis.

The processes involved in this type of investigation are similar to those found in both the observational and experimental investigations.

The process of investigation by survey

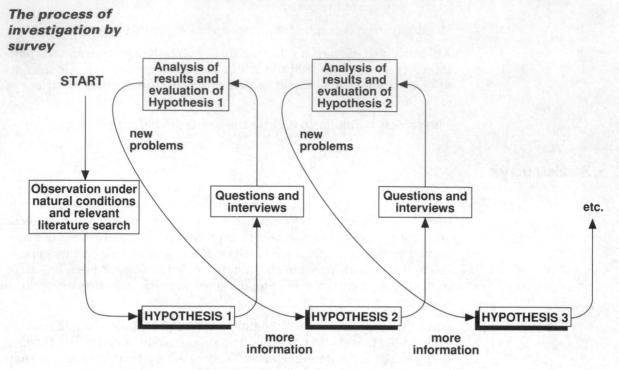

From these flow diagrams you will see that investigating is very much a cycle, continually abandoning or modifying existing hypotheses and/or coming up with new ones.

Applying this model to the layout of a project we find that there are six main features which would be applicable to most investigations:

1. Choosing a topic
2. Literature searching
3. Designing the investigations
4. Preliminary work
5. The main investigation
6. Writing up the report

We will be looking at each of these stages in detail later.

3 Appropriate Techniques

3.1 SAFETY

It is essential that whatever you propose to do does not endanger yourself or anyone else. You could be working on your own and it is essential that you check with your teacher any safety implications with respect to the work that you are going to carry out. The hazards which could arise in the laboratory or during field work are too numerous to list in a book like this. You should therefore read the appropriate literature before starting the work and follow carefully the safety policy of the institution. A most useful guide is the CLEAPSS Laboratory Handbook produced by the CLEAPSS School Science Service, Brunel University, Uxbridge UB8 3PH. This includes HAZCARDS which are a quick reference. Possible dangers which may arise should be identified and safeguarded against. However, if you follow the normal safety procedures that you have learnt during your courses, the dangers should be minimised. Particular equipment and chemicals that you might use during a project but which you would not have come across during normal coursework require special care and consideration.

You should produce a **risk assessment** for *every* practical (experimental or observational) that you are going to carry out, even if it carries no apparent risk.

The guide on the next page should help you to complete a risk assessment form such as the one shown. All such forms should be included in your final report.

Remember that field work can present safety problems. For example, if you are working on an exposed coast in stormy weather you could get washed away or dashed against rocks.

> **1** What precautions should be taken to prevent this from happening?

3.2 SUITABLE ORGANISMS

There is of course a wide range of organisms available for study. Naturally you should select that organism which is most suitable. Suitability will depend on factors like availability, ease of maintenance, size, what your investigation is about, etc.

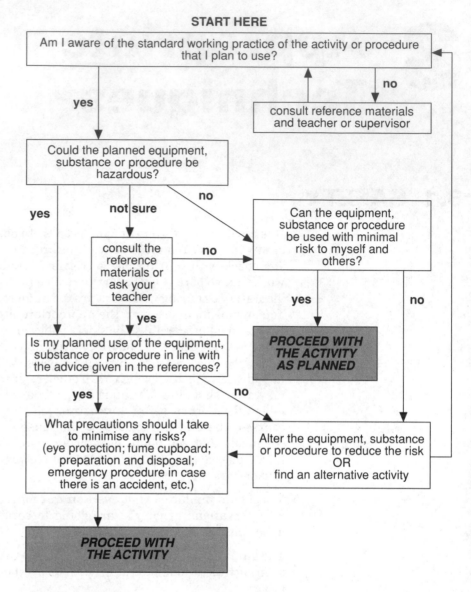

START HERE

Am I aware of the standard working practice of the activity or procedure that I plan to use?

yes | **no** → consult reference materials and teacher or supervisor

Could the planned equipment, substance or procedure be hazardous?

yes | **not sure** | **no**

consult the reference materials or ask your teacher

no → Can the equipment, substance or procedure be used with minimal risk to myself and others?

yes → **PROCEED WITH THE ACTIVITY AS PLANNED**

no →

Is my planned use of the equipment, substance or procedure in line with the advice given in the references?

yes | **no**

What precautions should I take to minimise any risks? (eye protection; fume cupboard; preparation and disposal; emergency procedure in case there is an accident, etc.)

Alter the equipment, substance or procedure to reduce the risk OR find an alternative activity

PROCEED WITH THE ACTIVITY

INVESTIGATION: RISK ASSESSMENT FORM

Title of investigation: _____

Type of activity (experiment, field work, etc.): _____

Details of activity: _____

_____

Hazardous equipment, substances, activity (for each detail the possible risk): _____

Safety measure to be used (containment, ventilation, heating method, etc.):_____

Risk assessment (describe your work methods): _____

_____

Methods of disposal of hazardous materials: _____

Emergency procedure in case of an accident: _____

Signed by student _____

Signed by teacher _____

3.2.1 Microorganisms

These include bacteria, fungi, yeasts and protozoa, and provided that you use microorganisms that are not pathogenic (disease-causing) there should be few problems. Since they are very tiny they don't take up much room (always at a premium for project work), they reproduce rapidly and feeding is not a major problem. Often however you will have to use microscopy. You must be well versed in aseptic techniques otherwise your experiments will become contaminated.

Information regarding the kinds of microorganisms to use, safety in handling them and the principles of good practice are all contained in the useful booklet produced by the Department of Education and Science, *Microbiology, an HMI guide for schools and further education* (HMSO 1990 with amendments).

3.2.2 Plants

Plants are very suitable organisms for investigations. There is a wide range of plants readily available for study; they are easy to grow, either from seed or cuttings; they can be put under a variety of conditions; above all, they are relatively harmless.

Plants are suitable for a wide range of experiments such as germination, growth, photosynthesis, respiration and transpiration.

Some people may however be allergic to pollen, to certain hairy plants and others.

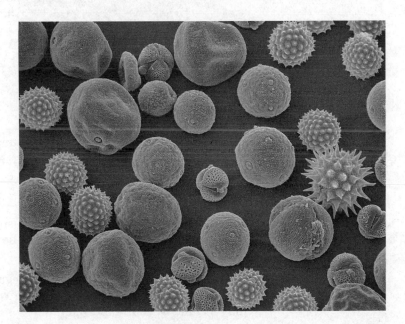

3.2.3 Animals

All animals must be kept in a healthy state. The legal position for vertebrate animals is that under no circumstances should they be subjected to any experiment or procedure liable to cause pain, stress, interference or departure from the animal's normal condition or well being. This must be adhered to strictly. Similar care and consideration should be given to invertebrates.

It is important that you should not carry out any objectionable experiments which are sometimes suggested as suitable for projects. All stock must be kept in a healthy state, being well fed and watered and kept in a clean condition. No experiments must be carried out that inflict any pain or distress.

Invertebrates

A wide range of invertebrates, often taken from the wild, are suitable for a variety of projects in behavioural, physiological and reproductive studies. Insects, for example beetles, caterpillars, butterflies and moths, can readily be obtained by using a variety of methods such as pitfall traps, light traps, etc. The fruit fly *Drosophila* is of course suitable for breeding experiments; locusts and stick insects are easily maintained – all of these might already be available in your institution. Some people are allergic to insects, which may be a problem. Woodlice (crustaceans) are perhaps the easiest to obtain and maintain. Molluscs are common on seashores and there is a wide variety of invertebrates found in the soil, in ponds and in streams.

Vertebrates

Consider what animals are kept in your institution since these will have been obtained from an accredited dealer. A variety may be available if there is an animal house on the premises, for example African clawed toads, fish, mice, rats, gerbils and hamsters. Such animals must be kept scrupulously clean and be fed regularly – remember about weekends and holidays! No wild mammals or birds, dead or alive, should ever be used because many of them carry diseases which can be transmitted to humans. (See CLEAPPS Section 14.)

Your teacher will advise you on any legal or ethical problems you might encounter, making sure that no harm will come to any animal that you may include in your experiments.

3.2.4 Humans

You might want to use your fellow students as subjects for your investigation, particularly if you are studying human or social biology. They are of course readily available, and investigating humans is interesting and relevant. Be careful however of any experiments where you might put them under stress, and be aware of any medical conditions that might make a particular experiment inadvisable. Your teacher should be able to help you here.

Beware of investigations of a psychological nature since these can be very difficult to carry out. Wherever possible devise an investigation where the variable under consideration can be measured clearly and is as objective as possible.

Humans are of course the only subjects if you intend to use questionnaires and interviews! In such situations you can obtain opinions and be more subjective.

3.3 MEASUREMENT

3.3.1 Units of measurement

Since we want to quantify the characteristics of organisms, counting and measuring will be important. Volume 2 in this series describes various methods of counting and measuring but you should know something about the metric system of SI (Systeme International) units since this is what all biologists use.

The SI system works by having a base unit for each physical quantity (e.g. metre, kilogram) and a prefix which tells you how many times the base unit is multiplied or divided. The main prefixes you will come across are shown in the table below.

Prefix	Symbol	Multiple
kilo	k	$\times 10^3$ ($\times 1000$)
hecto	h	$\times 10^2$ ($\times 100$)
deci	d	$\times 10^{-1}$ ($\times 0.1$)
centi	c	$\times 10^{-2}$ ($\times 0.01$)
milli	m	$\times 10^{-3}$ ($\times 0.001$)
micro	µ	$\times 10^{-6}$ ($\times 0.000\ 001$)

You will see that with the SI system we use **standard form**, which gives multiples to the power of 10 (e.g. 10^3 and 10^{-3}). This makes calculations and comparisons much easier than **actual form**, with which you will already by familiar (e.g. 1000 and 0.001).

Some examples of metric units you are likely to come across are shown in the following table. You will see that volume is sometimes described in two ways: the SI system uses cubic metres as its base unit, but conventionally litres are used when measuring liquids.

Quantity	Unit	Symbol	Standard form	Useful conversions
Length	kilometre metre centimetre millimetre micrometre	km m cm mm μm	10^3 m 10^1 or 1 m 10^{-2} m 10^{-3} m 10^{-6} m	1 km = 1000 m 1 m = 100 cm 1 cm = 10 mm 100 mm = 1 m 100 000 μm = 1 m
Mass	kilogram gram milligram microgram	kg g mg μg	10^3 g 10^1 or 1 g 10^{-3} g 10^{-6} g	1 kg = 1000 g 1 g = 1000 mg 1 mg = 0.001 g 100 000 μg = 1 g
Area	square kilometre hectare square metre square centimetre square millimetre	km^2 ha m^2 cm^2 mm^2	10^6 m^2 10^5 m^2 1 m^2 10^{-4} m^2 10^{-6} m^2	[1 km = 10^3 m, so 1 km^2 = $(10^3)^2$ or 10^6 m^2]* 100 ha = 1 km^2 1 ha = 2.47 acres 1 m^2 = 1000 cm^2 [1 cm = 10^{-2} m, so 1 cm^2 = $(10^{-2})^2$ or 10^{-4} m^2]* 1 mm^2 = 0.000 001 m^2
Volume	cubic metre cubic decimetre litre cubic centimetre millilitre cubic millimetre	m^3 dm^3 l or L cm^3 ml mm^3	1 m^3 10^{-3} m^3 10^{-3} m^3 10^{-6} m^3 10^{-6} m^3 10^{-9} m^3	1 m^3 = 100 000 cm^3 1 dm^3 = 0.001 m^3 = 1 litre 1 litre = 1000 ml = 1 dm^3 [1 cm = 10^{-2} m, so 1 cm^3 = $(10^{-2})^3$ or 10^{-6} m^3]* 1 ml = 10^{-3} litre or 1 cm^3 [1 mm = $(10^{-3})^3$ or 10^{-9} m^3]*

* See page 32 for an explanation of how to make calculations using standard form if you are not familiar with this.

3.3.2 Improving measuring

In order to make measurements easy and accurate:

1. Choose units that are convenient and easy to use. You would not express the length of a table in kilometres, nor the weight of a person in milligrams.

2. Choose a scale that offers the number of subdivisions necessary to give the accuracy that you require.

3. Read the scale to the nearest subdivisions. It is often possible to estimate points between the subdivisions of the scale, but estimates to more than one decimal place are likely to be of little use.

4. When numbers are added, subtracted, multiplied or divided, remember that *the answer is no more accurate than the least accurate measurement.* Beware of many places of decimals when you use a calculator – always round off to the nearest accurate measurement.

Suppose that you measured the heights of 100 bean plants with a metre rule, the smallest divisions of which were in centimetres. As you made the readings, you estimated the heights to the nearest millimetre. You then summed the heights and found the total to be 1953.4 cm. The arithmetic mean would be 19.534 cm, but you would be stretching the limits of accuracy to say that you could tell the difference between 19.4 and 19.6 on your measuring scale. The figure should be rounded off to the nearest one decimal place.

5. When rounding off numbers the normal convention (assuming that there is a fairly large number of observations involved) is:

Round *up* when the figure following is *above* 5; round *down* when the figure following is *below* 5.

> **1** Round off the following to one decimal place
>   (i)   46.746
>   (ii) 23.382
>   (iii) 5.973 486

What happens if the figure is 5; do you round up or down? The convention is to round *up* when the figure before the 5 is *odd*; round *down* when the figure before the 5 is *even*.

In the long run, about an equal number of such observations will be rounded up as are rounded down, so that no bias will be introduced.

> **2** What would 67.35 be rounded off to?
>
> **3** What would 66.85 be rounded off to?

3.4 STANDARD FORM

3.4.1 The standard form of numbers

In the table opposite you will see that numbers are given in what is known as the **standard form.**

Often in science we deal with measurements which involve very small or very large numbers, so that they contain a lot of zeros and make calculating difficult and prone to errors. This problem is overcome by converting numbers to standard form, which consists of two parts:

1. a number between 1 and 10, and
2. a power of 10.

Example 1

Convert the number 3 750 000 to standard form.

The first part of the standard form will be 3.75 (between 1 and 10) obtained by simply removing the zeros and putting in a decimal at the appropriate place.

We now determine how many times we have to multiply 3.75 by 10 to get back to the number given. In this example it would be six times, since the decimal place was moved six places to the right, or in other words, the difference between 3 750 000 and 3.75 is six decimal places.

The standard form of 3 750 000 is therefore 3.75×10^6.

Example 2

For a small number, for example 0.000 000 027 1 the procedure is just the same. We begin by putting down 2.71 – the first part of the standard form. In this case we have to divide by 10 a certain number of times to obtain the given number. We need to divide by 10 eight times since the decimal place is moved eight places to the left.

The standard form of 0.000 000 027 1 is therefore 2.71×10^{-8}. Notice the minus sign before the power.

1 Express the following in standard form:
    (i) 2500
    (ii) 0.005 6
    (iii) 6 000 000
    (iv) 0.000 017
    (v) 233.8
    (vi) 1000

With a bit of practice and use, you should find it quite easy to convert numbers to standard form.

3.4.2 Calculations in standard form

Given the numbers are in standard form, how do we calculate using them? It is actually easier to calculate in standard form, as you will have seen in the table of metric units on page 30.

Example 1

Calculate $(1.5 \times 10^4) \times (3.1 \times 10^8)$

The order of multiplying doesn't matter. We can rewrite the expression simply as

$(1.5 \times 3.1) \times (10^4 \times 10^8)$.

Multiplying 1.5 by 3.1 gives 4.65.

10^4 is $(10 \times 10 \times 10 \times 10)$ and 10^8 is $(10 \times 10 \times 10 \times 10 \times 10 \times 10 \times 10 \times 10)$.

Adding up all the tens we have 12 in total, that is, the sum of the powers 4 and 8:

$10^4 \times 10^8 = 10^{12}$, so

the standard form is therefore 4.65×10^{12}.

Example 2

Calculate $(2.71 \times 10^{-6}) \times (8.4 \times 10^4)$

Rewrite as $(2.71 \times 8.4) \times (10^{-6} \times 10^4)$

$2.71 \times 8.4 = 22.764$

$10^{-6} \times 10^4 = 10^{-2}$ $(-6 + 4 = -2)$

We now have 22.764×10^{-2}, but 22.764 is not between 1 and 10.

We rewrite 22.764 as 2.2764×10, so the answer is

$2.2764 \times 10 \times 10^{-2} = 2.2764 \times 10^{-1}$.

So, when *multiplying* powers of ten we have to *add* the powers.

Example 3

Calculate $\dfrac{(8.4 \times 10^6)}{(2.9 \times 10^4)}$

Rewrite as $\dfrac{8.4}{2.9} \times \dfrac{10^6}{10^4}$.

8.4 divided by 2.9 = 2.897.

$\dfrac{10^6}{10^4} = 10^2 \,(6 - 4 = 2)$.

The answer is therefore 2.897×10^2.

3   Express the following in standard form:

   (i) $\dfrac{841 \times 0.0038}{262.4}$

  (ii) $\dfrac{0.000\,18 \times 0.017}{0.000\,006\,24}$

 (iii) $\dfrac{1.8 \times 376}{0.48}$

3.5   ERROR

When you make measurements you should be aware of any errors that are likely to be associated with the procedure. Errors can arise from:

1. The measuring instrument itself. Whether it is a simple ruler, thermometer or pipette, or a more complex piece of equipment like a balance or a pH meter, precision will depend on construction and calibration.
2. Even if the instrument is as accurate as can reasonably be expected, the accuracy of the readings will depend on the skill of the user. Apart from mistakes which can be made from misinterpreting scales, people vary in their ability to see. It is always better for one person to take all readings that are going to be compared.
3. The level of accuracy of the measuring instrument must be appropriate. For example, a thermometer normally used for measuring a wide range of temperatures would not be suitable for taking the temperature of the body.

Before you make any measurements it is therefore important to think about what level of accuracy is required and the use that you are going to make of the data you obtain. Such considerations will determine the design of your investigation, the readings to be taken and the way in which they are collected. Usually it is necessary only to measure to the nearest gram or millimetre. If your experimental design is relatively crude, it is simply a waste of time to take readings to say, three decimal places.

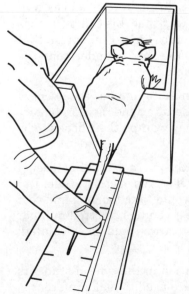

An important consideration occurs when measuring the lengths of parts of organisms, for example the length of tails of mice, or the arm lengths of humans. Where does the tail or the arm begin – how can we be sure that we have measured the same thing each time? We need to make a rule where we clearly define the limits so that measurements can be carried out consistently – they need to be defined so that others could carry out exactly the same measurements.

Always replicate (repeat) your measurement at least five times and from this calculate the mean (average). If you are taking a large number of measurements or readings try out the technique a few times to become more proficient and accurate, then discard these readings. Take as many readings as you have time for and for each data set calculate the mean, the variance and the 95% confidence limits. You can also visually represent the variation in readings by adding the confidence limits on a graph (see Volume 1 – *Dealing with Data*, page 84).

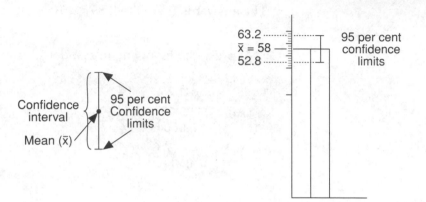

3.6 SAMPLING

A population, in biological terms, is made up of all the members of any specified group, for example, all the students in the UK; the flowers of a particular species in a defined area; the protozoa in a culture vessel; the limpets of a particular part of the shore, etc. Not all populations need to be large – some can be quite small, for example all the students in a particular institution; the mussels on a particular rock, etc. *It is the investigator who defines the population.*

Nevertheless the investigator often wishes to make inferences and comments about large populations. The only way that this can be done is to take small groups or samples from the population at random, so that inferences about the population can be made. You need to understand the relationship between a population and a sample.

Imagine that the publishers of this book wanted to find out the average reading level of A-level biology students or students attending introductory courses at university, presumably because they wanted their books to be as readable as possible.

It would be well nigh impossible to work out the average reading level of students from the total of *all* the reading level scores of *every* student in *all* the biology classes in the UK because it would take too long and cost too much. The reading test could however be given to a selected number of students and from this an average reading score could be calculated. This group of selected students is a **sample**.

There will, of course, be a great deal of variation in the type of students represented by this sample. When samples are used to make inferences about a population, it is essential that the individuals making up the sample must be representative of the population. If a sample is biased conclusions reached about that sample cannot be applied to the population.

There are a number of methods for selecting samples.

3.6.1 Systematic sampling

The items of the sample are chosen in a regular way, for example, every ninth item in the population. In our example *all* the A-level biology students in the UK make up the population, and depending on the time and money available, every 20th or every 100th student, for example, would make up the sample and be tested. Although simple, such systematic sampling techniques can be unreliable and may be biased by picking out regular variations.

Transects are a form of systematic sampling used to investigate transition from one habitat to another. They would be used for example for a survey of organisms on a rocky shore. Normally in such a situation a belt transect is used as shown:

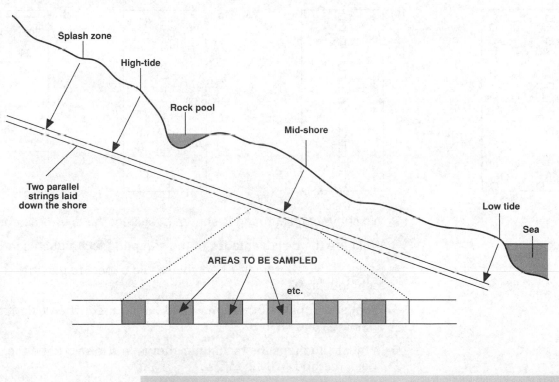

1 In what other locations would a transect be a suitable method of investigation?

3.6.2 Random sampling

The problems of bias in systematic sampling can be overcome by selecting the samples from a population in a random way. Various methods are used to obtain supposedly random numbers, for example using playing cards, dice, telephone directories, and throwing a quadrat frame over the shoulder. None of these methods is totally satisfactory, since the position of one sample depends to some extent on the position of the previous one. Only numbers generated randomly by computer or published in table form are completely independent of one another. The advantages of this method are that no prior knowledge about the population is needed, yet the sample will reflect the variation in the population.

3.6.3 Stratified random sampling

If the population includes a number of components, then the population is divided into these components and samples taken from each of the components. However, where possible the number of items sampled within each sample are in the same proportion as the total population. In our example, there are many components to the population – male and female students, urban and rural schools, first and second years of the sixth form, different types of schools, etc. The sample will contain students from the various categories in the same proportions as those found in the population.

The following diagrams represent different types of sampling. Each rectangle represents a field and each small square a sample site within the field.

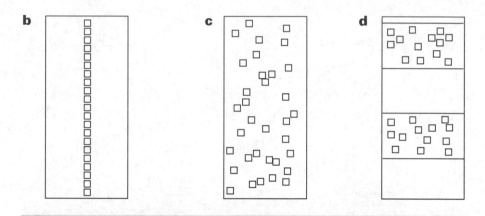

2 Which type of sampling is shown in each of the diagrams above?

3 What are the disadvantages of the sampling technique used in **a**?

4 Suggest two situations when you would expect to use the technique in **b**?

5 What additional information would be required when using the technique shown in **b**?

6 In most situations the technique shown in **c** is said to be the 'ideal' method. Why is this so?

7 Under what circumstances would it be best to use technique **d**?

EXERCISE

Farmer McLeod had a lot of problems with thistles growing in his fields. He bought a selective herbicide to treat a few of his fields. Since he was a canny chap, he did not treat all his fields – he wanted to compare treated with untreated fields in order to find out if the herbicide was actually killing off the thistles.

A   **B**

Figures **A** and **B** are scale drawings of two of McLeod's fields located close to each other on his farm (larger versions of these diagrams are given on pages 138 and 139). During the previous year field **B** was treated with the herbicide while field **A** was not treated (the control for comparison). The dots on each of the diagrams represent the positions of the individual thistles now present in the fields.

In order to determine if the herbicide had any significant effect on the thistles, both fields **A** and **B** have to be randomly sampled. (This is a paper exercise to show the principles involved – the actual activity could be carried out with quadrat frames in real fields.)

- Over each of the scale drawings of the fields draw a square of side 10 cm so that it fits as closely as possible around each field.

- Mark off every 5 mm on the 10 cm lines drawn and complete the grid of squares, each 5 mm × 5 mm.

- Starting as you would with a normal graph, label the lines of the grid that you have drawn, beginning in the lower left-hand corner with 00, 01, 02, 03, 04, 05, 06, 07, 08, 09, 10...19 on the X axis and the same for the Y axis.

- Using the table of random numbers given below or generating a set of random numbers on the institute computer (your teacher/lecturer will tell you how if you don't know) select pairs of numbers from the list – going in any direction that you choose (i.e. across from left to right; across from right to left; down or up – it doesn't matter).

12 07	13 09	07 07	03 11	03 09	17 07
00 15	16 11	15 17	11 03	17 02	06 11
04 03	04 19	11 04	15 19	08 07	00 02
00 18	03 03	15 06	19 13	11 04	07 19
18 11	04 01	07 09	06 10	05 10	04 11

- Starting with field **A**, use each pair of numbers as coordinates to identify a square on the grid that you have drawn. The first number of the pair of numbers identifies the position on the X (horizontal) axis and the second number of the pair the position on the Y axis. Where the two lines cross should be used as the lower left-hand corner of the sample quadrat.

(i) If the square identified has already been sampled, then reject it and repeat the selection process with the next pair of numbers.

(ii) If the full area of the square identified is not occupied by the field, then reject it and repeat the selection process with the next pair of numbers.

(iii) Count the number of 'weed' plants in each of the sample quadrats identified. A standard counting method should be used to avoid counting the same plant twice. An example of counting yeast cells using a haemocytometer is given in Volume 2 (page 114).

(iv) Record all the information about each of the quadrats in a table with the following headings:

	Field A		Field B	
Quadrat	Coordinates	No. of weeds	Co-ordinates	No. of weeds

(v) From the data calculate:
(a) the mean density of weeds per quadrat, for each field, and
(b) the variance of the sample of each field.

(vi) Using the statistical tests that you know (see Volume 1) determine if the herbicide had any significant effect on the population of weeds in field **B**.

3.6.4 Sample size

What size should the sample be? That is really determined by the time that is available for the work. Remember however that once you get going on your measuring, counting or whatever, you will quickly become more efficient and accurate at it. Counting and measuring large numbers of objects is the tedious and repetitive part of investigative work, so you will inevitably devise ways and means of speeding things up – you will probably set up some sort of 'production line' system, which not only improves efficiency but will also improve accuracy.

To carry out a statistical analysis of your results would require about 30 readings per sample for a t test; for a χ^2 test you should have at least five values for each box. (See Volume 1 *Dealing with Data* for details of the tests.) There are statistical techniques which can be used to indicate the ideal sample size, based on the results of a pilot study. A suitable text on statistics will supply the required information if you are interested.

In theory a sample which consists of a large number of small samples (sub-samples) is more accurate than a sample made by taking a small number of large sub-samples. Consider the two diagrams **a** and **b** on the next page where the same total area is sampled in each.

8 What reasons can you suggest for saying that the situation in **b** is 'better' than the situation in **a**?

9 Although the two strategies sample the same area, the area is not bounded by the same length of edge.
(i) Which has a larger edge bounding the area?
(ii) Why might this be a disadvantage?
(iii) What procedure has been used to partially overcome this problem?

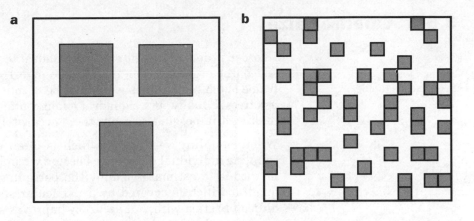

a   b

A large number of sub-samples inevitably requires increased time and effort. A number of sample units, N, must therefore be a compromise between the theoretical requirements and the time, effort and resources available.

The problem is therefore, when do you know that you have sufficient available data? How can the size of N required in a particular situation be predicted? There are two quite different questions here, although they are linked.

Imagine a student sampling blue-rayed limpets (*Patina pellucida*) from different seashore sites. Initially the student wants to be able to predict how many samples would be required to estimate satisfactorily the mean length of this species. In such a situation a pilot study is necessary, but what size should it be? A good general rule is that a sample using random quadrats should contain at least five units and preferably ten.

The measurements which the student obtained from the pilot study are shown in the table.

Lengths of *Patina pellucida* mm				
7.46	6.29	6.27	10.29	6.76
9.14	9.25	6.10	7.88	4.79

Using this type of data from a pilot study, there are several statistical methods which can be used to produce an estimate of a satisfactory sample size. The simplest method is based on the formula for determining the Standard Error of the Mean:

$$\mathrm{SE}\bar{x} = \frac{s}{\sqrt{N}}$$ where s = standard deviation and N = number in sample

We can say that a sample, drawn at random for a normally distributed population (see Volume 1 page 84) will have a probability of 0.95 (95%) of falling within the range $\bar{x} \pm 1.96 \times \dfrac{s}{\sqrt{N}}$.

3.6.5 Quadrat size

In order to determine the size of a quadrat to be used, firstly consider the size of the organism you are going to investigate. The standard quadrat frame of 0.5 metre sides would not be of much use if you were sampling oak trees! Equally such a quadrat might contain 20 000 to 30 000 barnacles, making it impossible to count them accurately.

When sampling vegetation which is often extensive and interwoven, counting individual plants can become virtually impossible. The simplest method is to estimate visually the percentage of each randomly placed quadrat which is covered by a particular species of plant. This can be difficult to start with, but accuracy improves with practice. Several scales have been developed which improve the efficiency and accuracy of such methods.

Two commonly used cover-abundance scales are the Braun-Blanquet and Domin Scales:

Braun-Blanquet scale	
Cover more than 75% of the area	5
Cover 50–75% of the area	4
Cover 25–50% of the area	3
Very numerous, covers at least 5% of the area	2
Plentiful but small cover value	1
Sparse or very sparse	+
Absent	−

Domin scale	
Cover about 100%	10
Cover about 75%	9
Cover about 50–75%	8
Cover about 33–50%	7
Cover about 25–33%	6
Abundant cover c.20%	5
Abundant cover c.5%	4
Scattered; cover small	3
Very scattered; cover small	2
Scarce; cover small	1
Isolated; cover small	X

3.6.6 Point frame

The point frame provides a more objective technique for determining percentage cover of a species than the quadrat.

Although the point frame is most often used for investigations of plants, it could be used in other situations to increase accuracy.

When using the point frame the sites for its use may be determined using random numbers to give the coordinates of a grid. The detailed positioning of the point frame with respect to the randomly selected points is not all that important, but it should be consistent. The frame is placed on the ground with all the needles withdrawn. Each pin is then carefully lowered until it touches the vegetation. Recordings are made of the number of needles which make contact with the species being studied. The frame allows ten readings to be taken at each site so that a large number of readings can be accumulated very quickly, and from these a percentage ground cover can be determined thus:

Total number of readings = 1500 (10 points at each of 150 sites)

Number of pins in contact with species A = 132

$$\% \text{ cover of species A} = \frac{132}{1500} \times 100 = 8.8\%$$

> **12** In a survey using a point frame to estimate the percentage cover of a particular species of plant, the total number of readings taken was 10 points at each of 50 sites. The total number of pins found to be in contact with the plant was 244. What is the percentage cover of this species of plant?

3.7 NEAREST NEIGHBOUR ANALYSIS

If you examine the underside of sycamore leaves during the summer and autumn you will be almost sure to find a large green aphid (greenfly) *Drepanosiphum platanoides* living there. Their distribution on the leaf can be analysed using a 'nearest neighbour analysis'.

These diagrams represent different distributions of aphids on leaves.

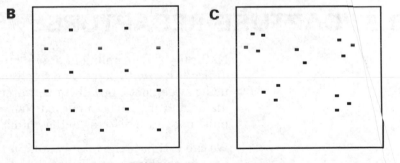

Each point represents the position of an aphid on the leaf. To illustrate use of this type of analysis carry out the following:

> **1** For each aphid in **A** measure in turn (to the nearest mm) the distance from one aphid to its nearest neighbour (start anywhere) and record this measurement (*r*).
>
> **2** Cross out the aphid for which the measurement in **1** was made.

3 Repeat the measurement for each aphid on the leaf, remembering to cross them out in turn.

4 Calculate the 'mean observed distance' r_A

where $r_A = \sum \frac{r}{n} =$ the sum of all the r measurements divided by the total number of aphids on the leaf.

5 Calculate the 'density' D of the aphids

where $D = \frac{n}{\text{leaf area}}$ (mm^2)

Leaf areas can be estimated using mm graph paper.

6 Calculate the 'expected mean distance' between nearest neighbours for this density of randomly distributed aphids on the leaf, r_E,

where $r_E = \frac{1}{2}\sqrt{D}$.

7 Calculate the ratio R, which is a measure of the degree to which the observed distribution departs from random,

where $R = r_A / r_E$

If $R = 1$ it indicates randomness,

if $R = 0$ it indicates aggregation, and

if $R = 2.15$ it indicates maximum spacing.

8 Repeat the calculations **1** to **7** for leaves **B** and **C**.

9 Comment on the pattern of distributions found in **A**, **B** and **C**.

This technique can be used to determine the distribution of a wide range of organisms in nature, and this in turn can lead to further interesting hypotheses which could be tested.

3.8 CAPTURE–RECAPTURE

Naturally the sampling of organisms which move around is much more difficult than with plants and sessile animals. A wide variety of techniques using sweep nets, pitfall traps, water traps, sticky traps, light traps and mammal traps can be employed. Remember however that any method used must not cause distress to the animals concerned.

We can estimate the total population of a particular mobile species in an area by catching a number of the organisms, marking all the individuals that have been caught and then releasing them. They should, in theory, then mix evenly with the total population. A second sampling of this population after a period of time should contain marked and unmarked individuals. From such data an estimate of the total population can be calculated using what is known as the Lincoln analysis, which assumes the ratio:

$$\frac{\text{Total population } (P)}{\text{Original number marked } (a)} = \frac{\text{Number in sample } (n)}{\text{Number recaptured in sample } (r)}$$

So that the total population $P = \dfrac{a \times n}{r}$

For this equation to be true the following conditions have to be assumed:

1. The marking method must not affect the animal.
2. The mark will remain throughout the duration of the investigation.
3. The marked individuals mix thoroughly with the total population before being recaptured.
4. The likelihood of an animal being recaptured must not change with age.
5. The population is a closed one – no immigrants or emigrants.
6. There are no births or deaths during the period of the investigation.

Example

A student collected 172 isopods (*Ligia oceanica*) under stones high up on the shore. He marked these with a dot of paint on their undersides and released them. Twenty four hours later he collected 126 from the same area and, of these, 8 were found to possess a dot of paint. How many isopods were there in this area?

Total population = original number marked multiplied by the number caught in second sample divided by the number marked in the second sample, i.e.

$$172 \times \frac{126}{8} = 2709 = \text{estimated number in population.}$$

> **1** In an investigation on a population of earwigs, 84 were caught in pitfall traps. These were marked on the underside with a spot of paint and released. In a second trapping a week later, 102 were caught and of these 12 were marked. What is the estimated total population of earwigs?

3.9 EQUIPMENT

Naturally you would wish to use the best equipment available to you. You should, where possible, use what is available in your institution. Good work doesn't always need sophisticated equipment – you can produce excellent work with a minimum of equipment. If something suitable is not available you could design and build your own if you are so inclined.

There are nevertheless certain items of equipment which are readily available and these can be used to good effect in a multitude of ways. The following can be used to produce meaningful data.

3.9.1 The microscope

The microscope is synonymous with biology. You may, in the course of an investigation, wish to examine, count or measure very tiny objects, parts of organisms, etc. and so they need to be magnified.

A range of magnifications is available, from a hand lens magnifying ×10, to a stereomicroscope of around ×20, to a monocular light microscope magnifying up to ×1000. Although an electron microscope would not normally be available, electron micrographs are suitable for a range of investigations.

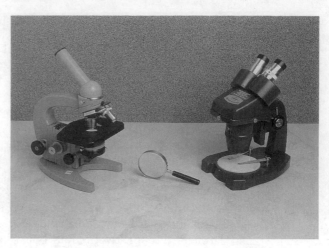

3.9.2 Measuring length

There is a wide range of measuring instruments and it is important to select the appropriate instrument for the task.

If the objects to be measured are extremely small, then the microscope may be used. Measuring using a microscope is known as micrometry, and this is fully described in Volume 2 pages 140, 144 and 160.

If you want to measure to an accuracy of 0.1 mm then use a micrometer screw gauge or a sliding vernier caliper.

Measurements to within 1 mm can of course be made with an ordinary mm ruler – longer measurements with a metre rule.

Long distances can be measured using a long tape measure.

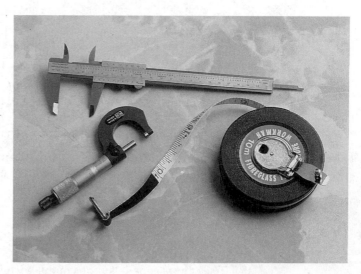

3.9.3 Measuring volume (liquids)

During the course of your investigation you may need to make up solutions and for this you will require accurate measurement of volumes. Graduated cylinders (of various sizes), disposable syringes (available in 1 cm^3, 5 cm^3, 10 cm^3 and 20 cm^3 sizes) and pipettes (range of sizes) are useful for this purpose. Always make sure to use a pipette filler instead of sucking up liquids.

3.9.4 Making up solutions

Making up solutions can be confusing since the concentration of a solution may be written in a variety of ways – moles per cubic decimetre, grams per litre, or as a percentage.

mol dm^{-3} (moles per cubic decimetre/litre)

Moles per cubic decimetre is the most common convention. You will often come across the term 'molar' (M) which is used in place of mol dm^{-3}.

The term mol dm^{-3} tells us how many times the molecular mass in grams (moles) of a chemical is dissolved in one litre of the solution. Take common salt (sodium chloride) as an example: the atomic mass of sodium is 23.0 and that for chlorine is 35.5, so the molecular mass of sodium chloride is 58.5. The molecular weights are normally given on the bottle containing the chemical. A mol dm^{-3} solution of sodium chloride would therefore contain 58.5 grams in 1 litre of water. (Remember that if you dissolved the 58.5 grams in 1 litre of water the final volume would be greater than 1 litre, so the salt is dissolved in less than 1 litre of water and this is then made up with water to 1 litre.)

To calculate the number of grams of the chemical needed to make up the final volume use the formula:

molecular mass of chemical × concentration required × volume wanted in litres (or ÷ 1000 for volume in cm^3/ml).

Example
Anhydrous sodium carbonate – on the bottle the molecular mass is given as 105.9. (Sodium carbonate is Na_2CO_3; atomic mass of Na = 23; atomic mass of carbon = 12; atomic mass of oxygen = 16. $(2 \times 23) + 12 + (3 \times 16)$ = 106, which is close enough for making up solutions.)

(a) If you wanted a quantity of the sodium carbonate solution which is different from 1 litre:
For 1 litre of 1 M solution you needed 106 g
For 2 litres of 1 M solution you would need $2 \times 106 = 212$ g
For 250 cm^3/ 250 ml of 1 M solution you would need $0.25 \times 106 = 26.5$ g (since 250 cm^3 = 0.25 litre)

(b) If you require a different concentration:
For 1 litre of 1 M solution you needed 106 g
For 1 litre of 2 M solution you would need 2×106 g = 212 g
For 1 litre of 0.1 M solution you would need $106 \times 0.1 = 10.6$ g

(c) If you required both a different concentration and volume, then adjust each in turn. If, for example, you needed 500 cm^3 or ml of an 0.5 M sodium carbonate solution:
For 1 litre of 1 M solution you needed 106 g
For 500 ml or cm^3 of 1 M solution you would need $106 \div 2 = 53$ g
For 500 ml or cm^3 of 0.2 M solution you would need $53 \times 0.2 = 10.6$ g

---

1 You wanted to make up 250 cm^3 of an 0.25 M solution of sodium hydrogen carbonate (atomic mass of H = 1). Calculate how many grams of the solid you would have to weigh out.

---

g l^{-1} (grams per litre)

Solutions in biology are often expressed in grams per litre (g l^{-1}). The power to the minus one just means per.

To make up solutions of a particular concentration simply take the number of grams of the solid as stated, dissolve in less than a litre of water and make up to 1 litre with water.

If you want less than 1 litre, simply multiply by that volume, e.g.

If you wanted 250 ml of a 10 g l^{-1} solution you would weigh out $(10 \times 250) \div 1000$ g of the solid and make up to 250 ml.

Solutions as percentages

This simply indicates the number of grams of a solid in 100 ml or cm^3 of the solution, e.g. a 5% solution of sucrose would mean 5 grams of sucrose made up to 100 ml with water.

Be very careful if you are diluting concentrated acids. ***Acid should always be added to water, never water to acid***. Such dilutions are more complicated to make up and should be left to the teacher or technician!

3.9.5 The colorimeter

Many reactions in biology are identified by a change in colour, for example the blue–black colour when iodine solution reacts with starch. We might want to determine how much starch is present in a mixture. We could make up a set of known starch concentrations and visually compare our unknown mixture with them. Such methods are limited by the ability of the eye, the amount of light falling on the solution, internal reflection, etc. As individuals we vary in our ability to distinguish between colours and our performance may even change with time.

To overcome these difficulties we can use a colorimeter – an instrument which measures the intensity of coloured solutions. Readings are taken on a meter which is unaffected by the operator's vision or subjective judgement.

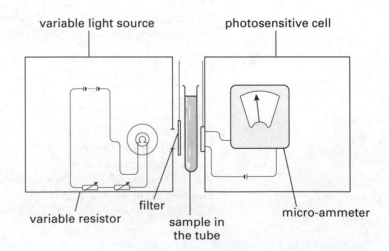

variable light source   photosensitive cell

filter   micro-ammeter
variable resistor   sample in the tube

The colorimeter consists of two main parts – a variable light source and a light intensity measuring device. The variable light source produces light, the intensity of which can be varied either by a variable resistor in the circuit, or by varying the width of an aperture through which the light passes.

The light passes through the coloured specimen under test on to a photosensitive element, which is connected to a micro-ammeter. The more intense the colour, the less light will fall on the photoresistor, and so the smaller will be the reading on the meter scale.

An important part of the colorimeter is the colour filter, and its function should be understood. A blue solution is blue because blue light passes through it while the other colours are absorbed by it. Blue light is therefore the least useful if we are trying to measure the blueness of a solution, and red light would be the most useful. For this reason a red filter is used in the colorimeter if we are measuring the density of a starch/iodine sample.

Often in biology measurements are required for a variable which can be very difficult or even impossible to measure directly using available equipment. The only way around such a problem is to find a variable which is relatively straightforward to measure and which is related in some way to the variable that is very difficult or impossible to measure.

As an example of such a situation, an investigation was carried out into the course of an enzyme-controlled reaction – the action of amylase on starch. To determine the course of this reaction it was necessary to quantify the amount of starch present, as a percentage, at particular times from the start of the experiment when the enzyme and starch substrate were mixed. Normally this would be extremely difficult to do. If samples were taken at different times from the start how could the percentage of starch in the mixture be determined? Since starch forms a dark blue colour with iodine/potassium iodide solution, a colorimeter was used to measure the optical density (intenseness of colour) of the mixture.

The amylase was mixed with the starch 'solution' and, at given intervals of time, samples were taken and iodine/potassium iodide solution added. These samples were placed in the colorimeter and readings taken. When this experiment was carried out the following results were obtained:

Time from mixing (min)	0	5	10	15	20	25	30
Colorimeter reading	0.1	4.2	21	39	58	82	100

These colorimeter readings are however relatively meaningless since they don't tell us what we want to know – the percentage of starch present. There is obviously an inverse relationship between the starch concentration and the colorimeter readings, since the more starch there is present the darker the colour will be, so less light will pass through the solution, and so the colorimeter reading will be lower.

In such situations the only way of overcoming the problem is to go from 'known' to 'unknown'. A series of *known* concentrations of starch from 0.5% down to 0.0125% were prepared by serial dilution. To particular volume samples of each concentration a particular volume of standard iodine/potassium iodide solution was added. Each sample was then placed in the colorimeter and readings taken. The results were as follows:

Starch conc. (%)	0.5	0.4	0.3	0.2	0.1	0.05	0.025	0.0125
Colorimeter reading	0	0.2	1.0	4.0	17	35	55	65

When these results are plotted on a linear grid it results in an exponential curve, as on the next page.

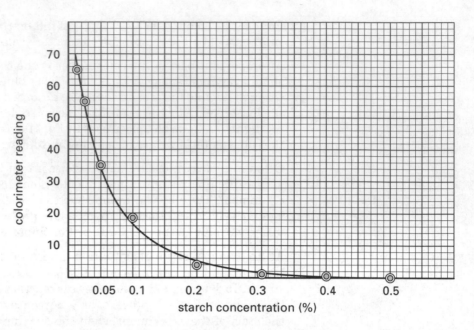

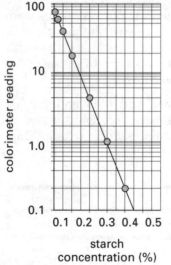

What we really want is a straight line, so the results are plotted on a log three cycle × linear grid. (For information on log graphs see Volume 1 page 22.) This makes drawing the graph line much easier and more accurate.

2 From the logarithmic graph, what would the starch concentration be if the colorimeter reading was 8?

The colorimeter readings obtained during the experiment can be converted using this graph (known as a conversion graph) into starch concentrations. These readings can then be used to plot a graph of the course of the reaction (starch concentration × time). Further information on conversion graphs is given in Section 3.11.

More recent colorimeters can provide analogue or digital readouts and can be used in conjunction with a computer – see section 3.9.7.

3.9.6 Agar wells

A relatively simple but effective way of studying enzyme activity is to use agar wells. Let us say that you wanted to investigate the effect of the concentration of amylase on starch.

Agar is made up to which starch is added and this is poured into Petri dishes in the usual way. When the starch/agar has cooled and set, round holes are made in it using a cork borer – these act as wells into which a particular volume of amylase is placed using a pipette. Each Petri dish, with say six holes, is allocated to a particular amylase concentration.

The amylase diffuses into the starch agar and breaks down the starch. After the plates have been left for a time (at the same temperature, etc.) iodine/potassium iodide solution is spread over the agar. Where starch is present it will turn blue–black, and where the amylase has digested the starch it will remain the brown–yellow of the iodine. 'Clear' circles will become visible around the wells. By measuring the diameters of these circles we get a measure of the activity of the amylase.

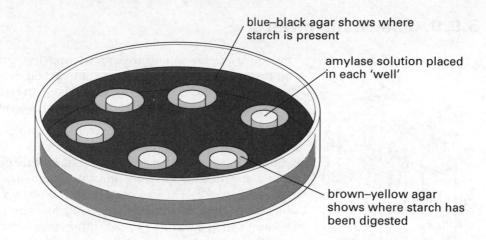

blue–black agar shows where starch is present

amylase solution placed in each 'well'

brown–yellow agar shows where starch has been digested

Such a technique can be used to good effect to investigate a wide range of variables on the activity of any number of different enzymes, using of course the appropriate substrate mixed with the agar.

3.9.7 Data logging

In recent years a range of sensors that can provide inputs suitable for interfacing with computers have become available. These have made the collecting of data much easier and have overcome the problems associated with regular collection of data at given time intervals, at weekends and during holidays. Such systems are also ideal for longer term data collection.

There are sensors which measure atmospheric pressure, humidity, light, conductivity, oxygen concentration, pH, pulse rates, sound and temperature. Sensors are also available which measure the position of an arm; there is also a strain gauge, a thermocouple and a manometer.

Such sensors are very suitable for project work and open up all sorts of possibilities for dealing with situations that were previously very difficult or even not available for investigation. The parameters can be set for recording and the data obtained from them can be printed out as graphs on the computer. It is possible to take readings of a number of different variables at the same time and to see how an experiment is progressing by viewing the graphs on screen as the data becomes available.

Details of how to use these sensors is supplied with them.

3.9.8 Use of spreadsheets

Data should be recorded in a table, preferably as the data is being generated. Using a spreadsheet on the computer to record the data eliminates basic errors which often occur when a table is drawn up on paper. If the format of the table given in the spreadsheet is incorrect then no graph will be drawn, or the graph drawn will not be the one expected.

The use of spreadsheets thus helps to ensure the proper design of tables and also enables graphs to be copied and pasted into the document of the final report.

3.9.9 The respirometer

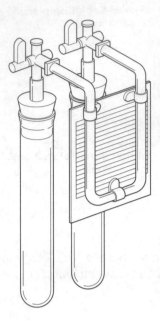

The respirometer is suitable for comparing the rates at which small organisms take in oxygen or give out carbon dioxide during respiration. It can be used, for example, for measuring anaerobic respiration rates in yeasts; to determine respiratory quotients in germinating seeds, etc.

Essentially the respirometer consists of two vessels (boiling tubes), one which contains the organisms while the other acts as a thermobarometer. Small changes in temperature or pressure causes the air in this vessel to expand or contract, opposing and thus compensating for similar changes in the other vessel. The two vessels are linked by a U-shaped capillary tube which acts as a manometer, enabling measurement of any changes in pressure which occur due to net differences between gas uptake and gas output.

Since aerobically respiring organisms give out carbon dioxide at the same time as taking in oxygen, we need to be able to measure both oxygen uptake and the carbon dioxide output.

Oxygen uptake

In order to measure the oxygen taken up, the carbon dioxide has to be removed as it is produced by adding concentrated potassium hydroxide solution to the tube in which the organisms are present. The potassium hydroxide absorbs carbon dioxide so any changes in the manometer levels will be due to the uptake of oxygen only.

Carbon dioxide output

This can be measured directly in anaerobically respiring organisms such as yeasts, but in aerobically respiring organisms they require oxygen to respire so we cannot remove it. Any change in the level of the manometer are thus due to the net difference between oxygen taken up and carbon dioxide given out. We can determine indirectly the amount of carbon dioxide produced by omitting the potassium hydroxide solution.

If, for example, the volume of oxygen absorbed is exactly equal over a period of time to the amount of carbon dioxide produced, there will be no change in the level of the manometer fluid. If, however, over a given period of time, say 20 minutes, there is an apparent production of 0.25 cm^3 of gas, this means that there was 0.25 cm^3 more carbon dioxide produced than oxygen taken up. When the potassium hydroxide was introduced, over the same period of time, there was a decrease in volume of 0.50 cm^3 – which tells us the amount of oxygen taken up.

Therefore we can conclude that:

the amount of oxygen taken up in 20 minutes = 0.50 cm^3

the amount of carbon dioxide produced minus
the amount of oxygen absorbed = 0.25 cm^3

the amount of carbon dioxide produced = the amount of oxygen produced
+ the amount of carbon dioxide produced – the amount of oxygen absorbed
= 0.50 + 0.25 = 0.75 cm^3

Remember that a manometer sensor is now available for this type of recording.

3.9.10 Modified Audus apparatus

If you want to measure the rate of photosynthesis you can use the production of oxygen as your parameter. This can be measured using the apparatus shown, but it is only suitable with acquatic plants. The rate of movement of a bubble along the capillary tube is an indication of the rate of photosynthesis. Remember that you often do not need to determine actual rates of photosynthesis, but only comparisons of rates under different conditions.

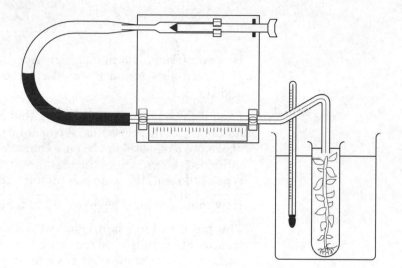

3.10 LATIN SQUARES

Imagine an investigation is being designed to find the effect of four different fertiliser treatments on the growth of a particular crop plant.

A plot of land is divided into four equal areas and each area will receive one of the four treatments before the seed is sown.

What way would you subdivide the area? Perhaps you would think that the following arrangement would be appropriate:

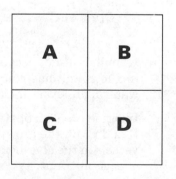

However, imagine that the land slopes from west to east so that the plants in A and C would receive less water than those in B and D, and this might affect their growth even more than the growth of the fertiliser.

To overcome this problem perhaps the plots could be arranged as follows:

A
B
C
D

However, imagine a line of high trees to the north of plot A so that the plants in plots A and B would receive less light than those in plots C and D.

Even if the environmental factors that are clearly recognised that would influence plant growth as, for example, the amount of water and light above, we could still not be sure that there were other factors which could influence the growth of the plants apart from the fertilisers, such as the type of the soil, the wind conditions – the list is endless.

How could the plots be arranged to take all eventualities into account?

The piece of land is divided into 16 plots (4 treatments ^{2}) and the treatments arranged so that each treatment appears in each row and in each column as shown. This is known as a **Latin Square**:

R	O	T	A	S
O	P	E	R	A
T	E	N	E	T
A	R	E	P	O
S	A	T	O	R

A 'Latin' or 'magic' square from an inscription on a fragment of wall-plaster found in a Roman house at Cirencester, c350AD

A	B	C	D
D	A	B	C
C	D	A	B
B	C	D	A

You can have any arrangement of a Latin Square – 3 × 3 or 5 × 5, etc.

1 Draw out 3 × 3 and 5 × 5 Latin Squares.

A similar situation can arise, for example in a glasshouse, where changes in the conditions can readily arise – the light might be variable, the watering uneven, the temperature might vary.

Imagine an investigation to find the effect of three mineral nutrients (A, B and C) on the growth of barley. The plants are to be grown in culture vessels in the glasshouse. It is decided that there should be five replicates of each nutrient.

What would be the arrangement of the 15 culture vessels so that all environmental factors, known and unknown, would not affect the experiment?

Look at the arrangement on the next page.

C	B	A	C	B
B	A	C	B	A
A	C	B	A	C

Would the system above be suitable?

2 Try to improve even further on this arrangement.

3 Imagine that you are carrying out an experiment on water loss from leaves by covering different surfaces of the leaf with jelly (which stops water loss by transpiration). You want to compare the following four different types of leaf form the same species:

A is completely green and non-variegated

B is from 80 to 90% green, the rest being yellow

C is from 50 to 80% green, and

D is less than 50% green.

Describe how you would arrange the treatments so that all the conditions are satisfied.

3.11 CONVERSION GRAPHS

Many items of equipment do not possess precise control knobs, for example incubators and ovens may only have an arbitary temperature control knob – this is of little use if we need to know the precise temperature. The control knob needs to be properly calibrated. This is a problem which applies to many different pieces of equipment.

All that needs to be done in the case of the oven is to place an accurate thermometer in the cabinet at specific control knob values and read off the respective temperatures. A graph is then drawn of control readings against temperature. If any particular temperature is required, the control knob reading can easily be read off the graph.

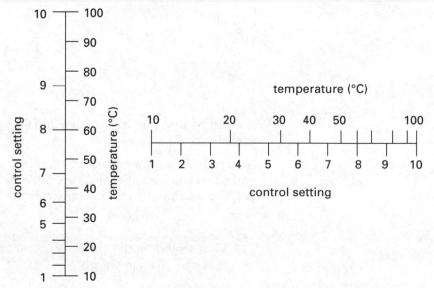

Another useful form of conversion graph is the **nomograph** (also called a nomogram or alignment charts). This is a computational chart which enable values of one or more variables to be converted into values of another variable.

Let us say that we wanted to find values of a variable which were difficult to obtain, but could be worked out from two easily measured variables. As an example, the surface area of the human body is extremely difficult to measure, as you could imagine.

In 1916 Dubois and Dubois worked out an equation which related the surface area to the weight and height of the body thus:

$$S = 0.007\ 184(W)^{0.425} \times (H)^{0.725} \quad \text{where}$$

S = surface area in m^2

W = weight in kg

H = height in cm

We could programme this into a computer so that by entering the height and weight variables, out would come the surface area. We can however simply use a nomograph as follows:

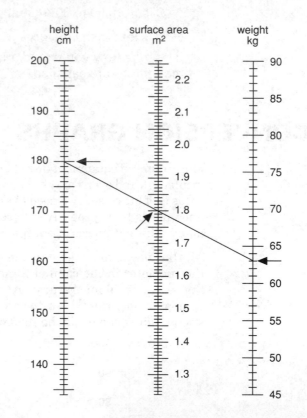

Example

If an individual was 180 cm high and 63 kg in weight, what would be their surface area?

A straight line is ruled between the two points – 180 on the height scale and 63 on the weight scale. This line intersects the surface area scale at 1.8. The surface area of this particular individual is therefore 1.8 m^2.

1 What would be the surface area of an individual who is 160 cm high and 75 kg in weight?

A useful variation of the nomograph can be used to estimate fitness in humans, using two easily measured variables. In the 'Step Test' subjects step on and off a platform 42 cm high at the rate of 30 times per minute. The order of stepping is – right foot on, both feet on, right foot off, left foot off (you can lead with left foot if desired). A stop-clock is started at the beginning of the exercise and the subject's effect is timed to the nearest second. If the subject fails to keep time over 20 seconds the exercise is stopped. The subject may stop voluntarily at any time. The exercise is ended after 5 minutes in every case. The subject then sits down immediately after the exercise and one minute later the pulse rate is counted for 30 seconds.

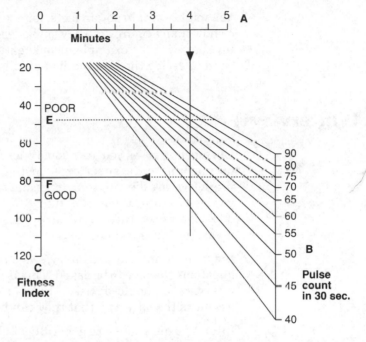

In a particular test, the subject managed to keep going for 4 minutes. His pulse rate at the end of one minute's rest was 75 beats for 30 seconds. A line is dropped vertically from the time line (A) at 4 minutes to intersect the pulse count line (B) for 75. From this point of intersection a horizontal line is projected across to the fitness index scale (C), and his fitness is read off. The lines F and E represent the upper and lower limits for most normal subjects.

2 Determine the fitness index of a subject who kept going for the duration of the test and, after one minute at rest, her pulse rate was 60 beats for 30 seconds.

3 In another test a subject kept going for only three minutes and, after one minute at rest, his pulse rate was 80 beats in 30 seconds. How fit was this person?

Think carefully as you go through your biology course and read your textbooks. Particularly pay attention to practical based books and all sorts of relatively simple techniques will be there that can often be adapted to suit your particular requirements.

3.12 SURVEYS

Surveys include collecting data about human activities using interviews and questionnaires.

If you are studying human or social biology you might want to carry out an investigation on human behaviour, opinions, characteristics, etc. People tend to be very unpredictable, being influenced by personality traits, circumstances and the environment. In such situations interviews and questionnaires are appropriate methods of carrying out surveys. They involve asking questions to which you want answers.

You might want to obtain facts, for example, what kinds of food people eat, or how many cigarettes they smoke each day. You might however want to find out why, for example, people eat chips or why they smoke. You will need to decide the best method of collecting the information you require.

3.12.1 Interviews

During interviews you ask people questions and record their answers either by marking on a sheet or by using a tape recorder. Remember that interviews are difficult to arrange and take up a lot of time. The information you get from interviews is likely to be more truthful than that from a questionnaire. Interviews are more useful if the situation you are investigating is complicated.

Before carrying out the interviews a schedule should be drawn up of the questions that are to be asked. This is important since all the people being interviewed should be asked the same questions to achieve consistency, as this is the only way that they can be compared.

Interview questions are generally of two main types:

1. Highly structured questions

These are specific questions, usually of a factual nature, to which there are clear answers. The responses can normally be recorded by ticking boxes, rather like a questionnaire. For example: How often do you eat fruit – once a day, once a week, occasionally, or not at all?

Responses to this type of question are straightforward to code, the categories being clear and unambiguous.

2. Open-ended, free response, general questions

This type of question allows the interviewee to respond in a variety of ways – they are given freedom to answer in whatever way that they wish. The interviewee is not prompted or led to a specific answer, but can be assisted by further elaboration if necessary. Such questions are generally used to find out people's opinions or attitudes. They should be worded in such a way that the answer is unlikely to be yes or no. For example: What influences the types of food that you eat? If a question is asked in such as way as to elicit a yes or no response (e.g. Do you think much about the types of food that you eat?) the interviewer can obtain further information by asking why they have answered yes or no.

Responses to this sort of question are often more difficult to categorise, since they can vary widely.

3.12.2 Questionnaires

Questionnaires are the most often used method for this type of survey. A questionnaire can be combined with an interview, or completed by the person answering the questions with or without the investigator being present.

The process of designing an interview or questionnaire is shown in this flow diagram.

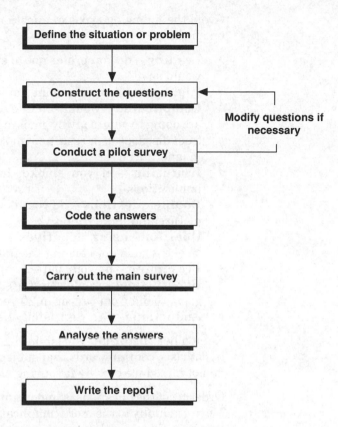

Define the situation or problem

- Prepare carefully by background reading and note any relevant points.
- Clearly write down your aims – what you are trying to find out?
- State your hypothesis clearly.
- State clearly the population which you are surveying.
- Decide how you will sample this population.

Construct the questions

Get a set of blank postcards and write out possible questions on these, since this makes the changing and later ordering of the questions much easier.

There are many types of questions which can be used.

- **Open questions** – where the answer can be a word, phrase or comment. Answers however have to be classified into categories for analysis which can be time consuming.
- **Lists** – a list of items is presented, any of which may be selected.
- **Categories** – a set of categories is presented where the respondent fits into only one, e.g. age group.

- **Ranking** – respondents are asked to rank a number of items in order of preference or importance.
- **Quantity** – response is a number giving the amount of a characteristic.
- **Grids** – a table or grid allows two or more questions to be answered at the same time.
- **Scales** – there is a number of different types, e.g. where there are simple categories (like yes or no); where the items are ranked (like strongly disagree, disagree, neither agree nor disagree, agree, strongly agree, etc.).
- **Statements** – can be given instead of questions.

Avoid the following types of questions: examples are related to a survey on smoking.

- **Leading** – do you prefer not to smoke because of the money that you would save?
- **Highbrow** – is emphysema caused mainly by smoking?
- **Complicated** – would you like to be told about all the harm that you are doing to your body by smoking, or shown videos of people suffering from diseases as a result of smoking, or would you just like to be left in ignorance?
- **Irritating** – if you smoke, have you considered the following implications?
- **Double questions** – do you like to smoke because it makes you feel mature and more friendly?
- **Questions using negatives** – do you agree that no person should smoke who is not earning the money to pay for it?
- **Presuming** – do your parents agree with your smoking?
- **Hypothetical** – would you stop smoking now if you knew that you were going to die from cancer in 20 years time?
- **Ambiguous** – are your family heavy smokers?

Remember also that you should ask questions which will test your hypothesis, contain words that subjects will understand, avoid jargon, and do not introduce bias by favouring one type of answer.

Ordering of the questions is important. Start with simple, factual questions. Move gradually to the more complicated questions and those which involve opinions. Finish with those that might cause embarrassment or hostility.

> **1** A questionnaire was designed by a manufacturer of tinned foods to be answered by housewives and the following questions were suggested:
> (a) What age are you?
> (b) Have you any children?
> (c) How much does you husband earn each week?
> (d) Make a list of the tinned foods in your house.
>
> Take each of the questions in turn and suggest how you could improve them.

Decide on a possible method of coding – rating scales, check lists or attitude scales, etc. (see next page).

You should now have a provisional draft for your interview or questionnaire.

Conduct a pilot survey

Try out your interview schedule or questionnaire on a small sample which is similar to the group that you are going to select as your sample for the main survey. Any serious faults are noted and the questions or their order changed, so that the interview or questionnaire is more effective.

Code the answers

Design a layout which allows answers to be recorded easily, by having a margin on the right-hand side of the page, spaced to correspond with the questions. Make your coding as simple as possible – converting the responses into numbers which can be analysed using a computer. The following is an example.

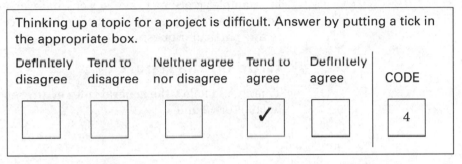

The code is 4 because it was the fourth box along that was ticked.

If the questions are open-ended you have to put the answers into categories – i.e. answers that are similar are grouped. You will get some idea of the categories from the pilot survey but further categories might have to be added when you carry out the main survey.

Finally, remember at the start of an interview or at the beginning of a questionnaire to:

- state the purpose of the survey
- thank those taking part for their co-operation
- assure them that the information they give will be confidential and that their name will not be connected in any way with the particular information they have given.

Carry out the main survey

Once the pilot survey has been completed and improvements made to the interview schedule or questionnaire, you must ask yourself some important questions before embarking on the main survey.

- Am I clear about the population that I wish to sample?
- What size of sample do I need?
- What sampling procedure will I use? (See page 34 for suitable techniques.)

> **2** 100 questionnaires were prepared for a human biology project on healthy eating habits in a school of 1000 pupils. In what way should they be distributed in order to obtain replies which are representative of the school?

Now carry out your main survey, not changing anything. You should finish up with your interview schedule or questionnaire with all the questions answered. You then code the answers according to your coding system.

Analyse the answers

You now go through all the interview schedules or questionnaires, and using a master sheet gate score the responses for each question. This will give you the total numbers of people giving particular responses to each question.

If you have access to a computer, the information can be put on to a database.

There are a number of ways of analysing the data depending on the type of question. For each question you can give the percentage of people who responded in a particular way and you can draw suitable graphs.

You can also compare the responses between different groups of people, for example according to age, sex or whatever, and using statistical analysis determine if there is any significant difference between them with respect to any particular questions.

Write up the report

This should follow the general rules of any report, and examples are given in chapters 6 and 7.

4 The Scientific Literature

4.1 LITERATURE IN SCIENCE

It is often said that it is as useful to know where to find a piece of information as to know the information itself.

In former days it was usual to believe that the older the authority the more reliable it was.

In the 1620s a monk who noted sunspots was told by his superior, 'You are mistaken, my son. I have studied Aristotle and he nowhere mentions spots. Try changing your spectacles.'

In his writings Francis Bacon (1561–1626) tried to dispel the reverence for authority and to get people to think for themselves. In 1605 he told the following fable:

> In the year of our Lord 1432 there arose a grevious quarrel among the brethren over the number of teeth in the mouth of a horse. For thirteen days the disputation raged without ceasing. All the ancient books and chronicles were fetched out, and wonderful and ponderous erudition, such as was never before heard of in this region, was made manifest.
>
> At the beginning of the fourteenth day, a youthful friar of goodly bearing asked his learned superiors for permission to add a word, and straightway, to the wonderment of the disputants, whose deep wisdom he sore vexed, he beseeched them to unbend in a manner coarse and unheard-of, and to look in the open mouth of a horse and find answer to their questionings. At this, their dignity being grievously hurt, they waxed exceedingly wroth; and, joining in a mighty uproar, they flew upon him and smote him hip and thigh, and cast him out forthwith. For, said they, surely Satan hath tempted this bold neophyte to declare unholy and unheard-of ways of finding truth contrary to all the teachings of the fathers. After many days more of grievous strife the dove of peace sat on the assembly, and they as one man, declaring the problem to be an everlasting mystery, because of a grievous dearth of historical and theological evidence thereof, so ordered the same to be writ down.

So much for relying on authority. We do not, however, want to reinvent the wheel. A literature search is a systematic search for published material on a particular subject so that you can gather valuable information on similar work that has been undertaken by others.

The volume of literature today in biology is phenomenal. How is it possible to find your way around the mountain of information that is available?

All of our biological knowledge results from peoples' observations and ideas. Any experiment, observation, or idea is interesting to the person who did the work, but it is not really a contribution to scientific knowledge until it is published for others to read, think about, or even repeat. Once published the work becomes a part of the scientific literature to which others who are interested in the same or related problems can refer. The experiments that are described can be repeated by someone else to find out if they get the same results or come to the same conclusions.

Most of the new scientific information and understanding results from the work of professional scientists. Today, as in the past, amateur naturalists and experimenters also make important contributions to biological knowledge.

4.2 SCIENTIFIC PAPERS

Scientists work on a problem until they think that they have something of interest and importance to report to other scientists. They then travel to specialised **conferences**, often in other countries, where they meet scientists working in the same or related fields. There they 'read' **papers** and put up poster displays which are concerned with their recent research work and are 'preliminary communications'. These are discussed with others and critical observations and suggestions are given. Once these are considered they then write (or rewrite) an article, or 'paper' which summarises their work and thoughts. This paper is then submitted to the editor of one of thousands of scientific **journals** published throughout the world.

Generally each journal deals with a particular field of science – the name of the journal usually gives a clue to the subject matter involved. In biology, for example, it is not difficult to tell what kinds of articles are to be found in *The Journal of Cell Biology* and *The British Journal of Nutrition*. In some cases the name of the subject matter is used as the title of the journal, e.g. *Ecology*, *Genetics*. Other journals carry the name of the society that publish them, e.g. *Transactions of the Royal Society*.

Other journals such as *Nature* publish articles of interest to scientists in all fields. Periodicals of general scientific interest include *Scientific American* and *New Scientist*. These review papers from the more specialised journals as well as carrying their own original papers.

Such journals are crucial since they record all the information and ideas that form the evolving body of scientific knowledge.

Scientists are very conscious of the need to register that they were the first to announce particular findings, since there can be disputes over who was the first to make a particular discovery. Journals therefore keep a careful record of the date when a paper is submitted and this date appears prominently if and when the paper is published.

Most papers begin with a very short **abstract** which is a summary of the paper. Then follows an **introduction** to the problem and includes references to earlier papers that relate to it. Then the **materials and methods** used in the work are described – usually in enough detail that the reader is able to evaluate the results or to repeat the experiments. In the next section the author reports the **results** in detail – data are listed in tables and/or graphs. Then follows a **discussion** of the significance of the work and the paper ends with a brief **summary** of the conclusions and a **list of references**.

The paper once submitted is sent by the editor to other scientists who are specialists in the field – these are known as **referees**, who are able to assess the quality of the paper and decide whether it is worth publishing or not. If it passes this review procedure the editor arranges to have it published in a forthcoming issue of the journal. If not, the paper is either returned to the author with the referees' reasons for rejecting it, or more commonly the author is asked to revise it in the light of the referees' comments and to resubmit it.

Refereed papers always have a much higher standing than non-refereed papers since they have gone through the 'fire of critical scrutiny'. This has its problems however, since if a paper is submitted which is truly new and imaginative, there will be no-one qualified to referee it. Excellent papers have been known to be rejected by respected journals and it was only years later that their importance was recognised. Authors do not normally know who the referees are but this could change in the future.

There is an artificiality about the research paper – since it misses out so much of what actually happens. The writer of an article for a learned journal leaves out all personal factors, mistakes and flashes of inspiration. Using the passive voice 'It has been shown that...' (s)he has to find coldly rational, logical reasons for performing a particular set of experiments and interpreting them in a particular way.

Scientific papers are full of jargon containing the sort of language that often only the specialists in a particular field understand. For example, the following is the Summary section of an article 'Specific Binding Sites for Corticosterone in Isolated Cells and Plasma Membrane from Rat Liver' from *The Journal of Membrane Biology* **120**, 201–10 (1991). Remember that most of the readers of such an article are conversant with the jargon and so it means much more to them than to others outside the specialism.

The specific binding of [^{3}H]corticosterone to hepatocytes is a nonsaturable, reversible and temperature-dependent process. The binding to liver purified plasma membrane fraction is also specific, reversible and temperature dependent but it is saturable. Two types of independent and equivalent binding sites have been determined from hepatocytes. One of them has high affinity and low binding capacity (K_D = 8.8 nM and B_{max} = 1477 fmol/mg protein) and the other one has low affinity and high binding capacity (K_D = 91 nM and B_{max} = 9015 fmol/mg). In plasma membrane only one type of binding site has been characterized (K_D = 11.2 nM and B_{max} = 1982 fmol/mg). As it can be deduced from displacement data obtained in hepatocytes and plasma membrane the high affinity binding sites are different from the glucocorticoid, progesterone nuclear receptors and the Na^+, K^+ -ATPase digitalis receptor. Probably it is of the same nature as the one determinate for [^{3}H] cortisol and [^{3}H] corticosterone in mouse liver plasma membrane. Beta- and alpha-adrenergic antagonists as propranolol and phentolamine did not affect [3H]corticosterone binding to hepatocytes and plasma membranes; therefore, these binding sites are independent of adrenergic receptors. The binding sites in hepatocytes and plasma membranes are not exclusive for corticosterone but other steroids are also bound with very different affinities.

Articles are written in an objective style whereby the scientist tries to remove the human element as far as possible – to include subjectivity is to include bias, or so the story goes. Scientific papers therefore give a false sense of objectivity.

It is perhaps because of this apparently 'cold' approach to writing that many young people are turned off science. We often hear nowadays of the concerns about so few young people showing an interest in things scientific. Perhaps the whole approach to scientific writing should be changed.

In contrast to the writing, the history of science is stimulated by human concern – reduction of misery, wiping out disease, drought, pestilences, etc. It is time that scientific papers were written in a style that projects some humanity and warmth even if there are a few warts. Scientists can actually be humorous and witty – why not give them the opportunities to be so if they wish? Referees and editors of journals are central to change – if their attitude could change then change would come since they do the selecting. On the other hand if *all* the scientists decided to submit papers for publication in a more human style, what could the editors and referees do about it?

You do not need to be so coldly objective when writing up your report. You can add as much of yourself into the scenario as you wish. Instead of writing '2 cm^3 of sodium hydroxide were added' you could write 'I added 2 cm^3 of sodium hydroxide', or instead of 'It was thought that' write 'I thought that', etc. Use personal instead of impersonal pronouns. Impersonal pronouns indicate no reference to any individual person so that the writing seems devoid of any human warmth or sympathy; it is cold and often dismal to read. There is rarely even a hint of humour. If you have a sense of humour then take the *occasional* and appropriate opportunity to use it.

The search for scientific knowledge recognises no national boundaries. Libraries subscribe to the journals of the world. One measure of the value of a library to scientists is the number of scientific journals to which it subscribes.

4.3 SEARCHING THE LITERATURE

How do you start to find the information that you are looking for? There are a few general principles which apply to most searches.

1. What exactly is the subject area that you want information on?
   Write this down as clearly as you can. Think if you are going to use an observational, experimental or surveying approach.
2. What depth or level of the subject are you interested in?
   Sources can range from encyclopedias, textbooks, reviews to original papers.
3. Use the sources as efficiently as possible, i.e. read the introduction and use the indexes.
   Obviously it is better to use computer databases if possible since these can help to speed things up.

4. Record all the relevant information.
   Obtain a set of postcards, one for each reference. If you want to find a particular publication you need to note:
   (a) *journal article* – Author(s), title in full, title of journal, volume, number, page numbers and date.
   (b) *book* – Author(s), full title, publisher, date and place of publication, edition and ISBN number.
   Since references must be properly cited in your report, such records are essential.

There are different libraries in which you could find useful background information. Some of these are readily accessible to you while others require considerable effort and motivation to find and use. It all depends what you are looking for, and the depth of background information you require.

4.3.1 School/college libraries

There is a hierarchy involved in searching for information about the topics you are interested in.

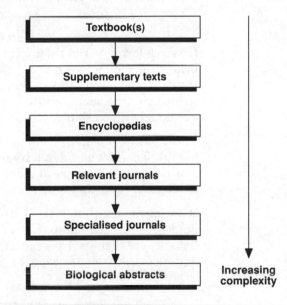

Textbook(s)

The first source to look to are your textbooks, but it is important to be prepared for errors even in 'authoritative' works. Textbook writers usually don't have the opportunity to read original papers or to carry out all the experiments, so they tend to reorganise the work of earlier writers. One can even find errors which are 'handed on' through generations of books. Your textbooks are nevertheless a useful reference for all sorts of topics. If you are interested in something that could form the basis of an investigation, look up the index, and if it is there check the relevant pages. You might get further ideas. Unfortunately few, if any, of such books cite references which would guide you to further reading on any particular topic.

You may have supplementary texts which cover particular topics in more detail, or deal with practical work. Often these can be excellent sources for investigation ideas. (The first two volumes of this series would be examples.)

Departmental library

The biology department of your institution could have its own small but specialised library, containing a range of books on different topics. Look through these to find if there are any on the topic you are interested in. You will usually find that these cite references at the back and these can start you down the road to a proper literature search. The departmental library might even carry some journals on biological topics.

The department should also stock copies of past investigations which are an excellent source for ideas.

Main library of institution

Your institution probably subscribes to certain publications which are important in the context of school science and biology in particular. Regularly published journals keep you up to date. *Nature, New Scientist* and *Scientific American* are the most common. Others are targetted at teachers – *The Biologist* and the *Journal of Biological Education* are published by the Institute of Biology while the *School Science Review* is published by the Association for Science Education. The *Journal of Biological Education* carries a section on practical biology.

The *Biological Sciences Review* is an excellent journal designed specifically for sixth formers and their equivalents. The editors state that 'it aims to bridge the gap between textbooks (which are often a year out of date by the time they reach the bookshops), science sections of the daily newspapers (which give the 'facts' but little 'theory') and the scientific journals (which are largely inaccessible to students).

These journals usually include reviews of articles or books which can be useful. The science department library or the main library of your institution should carry at least a few of these publications. They are full of ideas for investigation.

It is important that your institution carries identification guides, e.g. guides to the sea shore, life in freshwater, wild flowers, moths, trees, lichens, etc. These are essential to enable you to identify clearly the organism that you are working with.

4.3.2 Local library

Have a look in the nearest local library to find out what they stock. They usually have an excellent referencing section and may carry a number of books on biological topics.

Books in these libraries, like school and college libraries, are often classified according to the 'Dewey Decimal' system as follows:

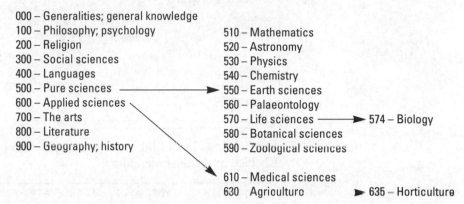

000 – Generalities; general knowledge
100 – Philosophy; psychology
200 – Religion
300 – Social sciences
400 – Languages
500 – Pure sciences
600 – Applied sciences
700 – The arts
800 – Literature
900 – Geography; history

510 – Mathematics
520 – Astronomy
530 – Physics
540 – Chemistry
550 – Earth sciences
560 – Palaeontology
570 – Life sciences ──► 574 – Biology
580 – Botanical sciences
590 – Zoological sciences

610 – Medical sciences
630   Agriculture ──► 635 – Horticulture

This system makes it relatively easy to find books in particular areas of interest since the shelves will be numbered in the Dewey System. If you look on an inside front page of a book you will find two useful numbers – a Dewey Classification number and an ISBN or International Standard Book Number.

The ISBN for this book is 0-7487-2048-0; the 0-7487 indicates the publisher is Stanley Thornes, the 2048-0 the particular book.

4.3.3 University library

If you want to delve deeper into your topic and live near a university, you might want to visit the library there to see what you can find. Universities have an 'online library catalogue' system on computer. When you go into the library (and one university may have a number of specialised libraries) you will find an array of terminals. They are very user-friendly – the one illustrated here is based on that at Queen's University in Belfast.

This is what is on the screen to start with:

```
        QUEEN'S  UNIVERSITY  LIBRARY

    WELCOME TO THE ONLINE CATALOGUE

    Press the RETURN key to begin
             your search
    (or E to exit and clear call)
```

Pressing the RETURN key brings up this on screen:

```
                    ONLINE LIBRARY CATALOGUE

Q  Quick AUTHOR/TITLE search     S   SUBJECT search
                                 B   Books you have on loan
T  TITLE search                  C   Classmark search
                                 H   How to use the catalogue
A  AUTHOR search                 L   Library news & information
K  KEYWORD in title search       N   Number search
         G GO to *JOURNALS* and other sub-catalogues
       E (at this menu) TO END SESSION and clear call
   Terminal set-up: see Library Information 110 for details
        Please select an option : THEN PRESS ENTER/RETURN
```

Let us press H to find out more about this catalogue. We press H then
ENTER and the screen shows:

```
               HOW TO USE THE CATALOGUE

The online catalogue (OPAC) contains records for all material
held in any of the Queen's libraries. At present there are
duplicate 'temporary' records for some items and these will
gradually be removed from the catalogue.

The following pages will give you some help in using the
catalogue. If you are not sure what to do, try looking up the
examples given for title, author, quick author/title, keyword
and subject search. Each kind of search has its own instructions
and a help screen to guide you.

If in doubt, ask one of the library staff.

N next page          E end help         THEN PRESS ENTER
```

This 'help' section continues for several 'pages' giving us advice on screen
about looking for a particular book, looking for a subject, finding material
in the library and what to do if it is not in the catalogue.

Let us try to find something under the Author Search. We go back to the
beginning and under AUTHOR search we key in A and the following
appears on screen:

```
                     AUTHOR SEARCH

Enter the author's surname followed by forenames or initials
(if known), separating the two by a comma
e.g.    FIRBANK, RONALD
        JONES, A.H.M.
Search for names starting with Mc under both Mc and Mac.
You may also search for corporate bodies, such as UNITED NATIONS
or BURROUGHS WELLCOME COMPANY.
------------------------------------------------------------------
NOTE: Authors may be shown under several different forms of
name - check backwards and forwards in the index to make sure
you find them all.
------------------------------------------------------------------
X display the author index              H for help
E to end enquiry                        THEN PRESS ENTER
 : GARVIN, J.W.
```

When we type GARVIN, J.W. the following information appears on screen:

```
                    ENQUIRY: Garvin, J W

There are 4 references for this author
-------------------------------------------------------------------
1    Skills  in  advanced  biology/Vol. 2/Observing,  recording
     and interpreting/1990
2    Skills  in  advanced  biology/Vol. 2/Observing,  recording
     and interpreting/1990
3    Skills in advanced biology/Vol. 1/Dealing with data/1986
4    Skills in advanced biology/Vol. 1/Dealing with data/1986


Select a line number to display more information

NN next author              X display the author index
PP previous author          E end your search
                                      THEN PRESS ENTER/RETURN
```

We now have all the books listed in the library under that author's name.

If we key in 3 (for reference 3) for more information we get:

```
  Reference number 3:

Garvin, J.W.
Skills in advanced biology, J.W. Garvin
Vol. 1, Dealing with data
Cheltenham, Thornes
1986
xi, 164p, ill, 28cm
Includes index
08595088x

LOCATION COPIES
Sci       1                    QH324 GARV

Press ENTER/RETURN to see the list of brief references
N next               X display the author index
P previous           L display loans
                     S other books on this subject
                     E end your search
                              THEN PRESS ENTER/RETURN
```

With this information we know that there is one copy of the book in the Science library, that it is to be found in the section coded QH324 GARV.

The online library catalogue can help you find a book if title but not author is known, it can suggest books in a subject, pick out key words in a quick title search, and much more. Used sensibly, it can save hours of fruitless searching – leaving you plenty of time to get on with your investigation!

University libraries also carry biological abstracts which list somewhere around 100 000 papers every year and help you to be able to find original papers. It is however unlikely, but still possible, that you might want to refer to these.

It is also good experience to visit and use a university library if you are intending to continue your studies at an institute of higher education. If you are already there, it is essential.

4.4 READING

Don't spend so long searching for information that you don't leave enough time for reading! To find what you want effectively first look through the contents at the front of a book, and scan quickly through the introduction. This will tell you whether it contains any information that is useful or not. If you find something which could be relevant look up the pages and scan rapidly through them and make any notes that might help. Once you learn to scan it is surprising how relevant points 'pop' out of the page.

You should have a few key words that are particularly relevant to your investigation which you can look up in indexes since this can lead you directly to an appropriate page.

Once you have found very relevant information, take your time to absorb the material and make detailed notes since these might be required for your discussion on the topic. Don't forget to write down exactly where you found the information – you need to be able to find a book or article easily again. It is really frustrating to have an important and very relevant note of something and not be able to find it again!

A full reference for a book includes:

1. the author or authors
2. the title of the book
3. the pages which are relevant
4. the publisher
5. city of Publication
6. date of publication
7. the ISBN number
8. notes: brief summary of relevant points.

For an article or paper write down:

1. author or authors
2. title of article or paper
3. title of journal
4. the volume and number of the journal
5. the date of the journal
6. the pages
7. any relevant notes.

You could make up a number of cards with these headings which you can carry around with you and fill in as required.

4.5 OTHER SECOND-HAND EVIDENCE

There are many other places where you can obtain information which might be relevant to your investigation. Organisations like charities, consumer councils and industrial enterprises often produce pamphlets and booklets giving useful information. Radio and television programmes can stimulate ideas and the BBC and ITV have education departments which will send you interesting materials (addresses given on page 130). Programmes like Horizon and Equinox are supported by written information. Magazines and CD-ROMs are other sources of useful ideas.

Always keep your eyes open for possible interesting areas that would lend themselves to investigation. You never know when they are going to crop up!

5 Planning Investigations

5.1 PROBLEM RECOGNITION

We have seen that the starting point of science is curiosity. Science is about being nosey, but not the type of nosiness that involves gossip or prying. It is simply wanting to know why things are the ways they are.

5.1.1 Imagining

Imagining requires the ability to visualise – to 'see' images in your head. It is a skill that requires continuous practice – just like everything else in life. When you have developed this skill it can be used for all sorts of things. Jack Nicklaus has stated that his golf swing is 95 per cent swing in his head and 5 per cent actual swing. Similarly, highjumpers mentally do the jump before actually doing it; racing car drivers mentally do a record lap; you can mentally prepare a meal, give a talk, mentally try to solve all sorts of problems, like why won't the car start. The list is endless.

We tend to observe the things that interest us and so we are more interested in the things that we ourselves observe – the problem, when perceived, then has a personal quality and a personal appeal.

Have a go at imagining. Imagine that you are looking out through a window on to a stretch of grass that has grown long and could do with being mowed. Then you think about the mowing – you imagine yourself mowing the lawn – actually imagine yourself pushing the lawnmower and even emptying the cut grass on to a compost heap. Then you begin to imagine and think in a wider sense – some people mow their lawns more often than others. Then your curiosity takes over and you wonder if mowing has any affect on the rate that the grass grows – would grass grow quicker if you cut it more often? Your mind then opens up this idea and asks – does hair grow quicker the more often it is cut? What about nails? If cows are milked more often do they produce more milk? All such ideas are worthy of investigation and could lead to important and relevant discoveries.

Then, as you look at the grass you see the daisies – are they evenly distributed over the lawn, or are they in clumps? Does the cutting of the grass have any effect on the growth of the daisies? Do the dandelions grow where the daisies are growing? Why do the daisies and dandelions grow where they do? There are patches of moss and clover. Why do they grow where they do? And so it goes on and on – there is no end to the questions that you can ask.

5.1.2 Problem solving

Problem solving is somewhat different from imagining. What do good problem solvers do that poor problem solvers don't do? Here are some ideas.

Good problem solver	Poor problem solver
• Thinks first • Clearly identifies the problem • Decides what needs to be achieved • Discusses a range of ideas and designs then selects the most promising • Listens to other points of view • Plans a course of action and carries it out • Has a method or purposeful approach • Asks 'can it be done better?'	• Rushes headlong into action • Doesn't identify the problem • Does not plan in detail • Makes repeated false starts • Doesn't listen to the views of others • Accepts inadequate results/solutions • Has no method or purposeful approach • Doesn't learn from mistakes

You have to be good at imagining and problem solving to be a good investigator, quite apart from all the other skills and knowledge that you have to bring to bear on the situation. Don't worry if you think that you are no good at such things – you will get better, but only if you try and keep practising.

My experience over the years indicates that students have three main problem areas when carrying out open-ended investigative work:

1. selecting a topic
2. keeping the investigation within bounds
3. procrastination – not getting down to the work.

Your project should be carried out when you are well into your course, when you can take a mature and disciplined attitude to the work.

5.2 SELECTING A TOPIC

Generally most students find that this is the most difficult aspect of investigative work. Some may even become obsessed with the difficulties, unable to make up their minds what to do. In such cases your teacher should be able to help you with prescribed lists of possible topics. If you have a lively and critical mind you should try to come up with ideas of your own.

I often used brain-storming sessions with my students where I fired questions at them to stimulate discussion, then by offering suggestions and ideas and bouncing ideas around, everyone ended up with possible areas to investigate. Discuss widely with your fellow students and others – you will actually find this an interesting experience.

Once you have selected a particular area of biology as a starting point, think up as many lines of inquiry as possible within the area in question. One main area can often spawn many ideas that are suitable for investigation.

Remember that your investigation doesn't need to be completely new, novel or earth-shattering.

Useful ideas can arise from:

- the course you are following
- other subjects you are studying
- past investigations
- examination papers
- books and journals
- television programmes and newspapers
- fieldwork
- where you live
- hobbies and other interests.

The course you are following

Certain topics might particularly stimulate your interest or whet your appetite. Ideas can also arise spontaneously during class discussions. You might like something to do with genetics, plant physiology, ecology, or human physiology for example. Some of the experiments which you have carried out could be extended to look at other variables or different organisms. Questions can arise that require answers.

Look carefully through your syllabus – at the topics, and at the knowledge and skills required, since during your investigations you will learn quite a lot of new knowledge, and develop skills that could be beneficial to you in your examinations, even your written examinations. Chapter 8 gives some ideas for possible investigations, based on coursework.

Other subjects

Think about the other subjects that you are studying, especially if you have a project to carry out in them as well – maybe geography, computer studies, technology, home economics, etc. You might find an investigation which could, with variations, be appropriate to two of them – at least the data could be obtained at the same time. They would have to be different since you will not be able to submit the same investigation for more than one subject, but you could look at different aspects. Even if you are studying art or music these can be fruitful areas for scientific investigation. It is often in the interface between two subjects that really interesting and innovative ideas can emerge.

Past investigations

If your institution has made a point of collecting past investigations as a resource then these are a mine of information, particularly if they contain a section titled 'Suggestions for further investigations' which have arisen during the course of the work (e.g. pages 115 and 123). Many of the suggestions are straight ideas for excellent investigations.

Examination papers

Look through past examination papers. These often give results of observational and experimental investigations which could be tried out in different situations or varied in some appropriate way. They will also highlight the knowledge and skills that can be best learned and reinforced during the course of investigative work. You will really know how to tabulate, draw graphs and understand statistical analysis when you do this with your own data!

The following question is from an AEB Paper (Question 19, Paper 1, June 1992) and would form the basis for an investigation. Note that actually carrying out an investigation also helps you to answer this type of question.

Two species of annual plant, A and B, grow naturally in the same habitat. You are asked to design an experiment to determine the effect of interspecific competition on the success of the two species. (Interspecific competition is competition between different species of organism.)

You are provided with five large pots, some growing medium and 250 seeds of each species.

1. (i) Complete the table to show how you would distribute the seeds between the pots.

Pot	Number of seeds of species A	Number of seeds of species B
1		
2		
3		
4		
5		

   (ii) Give the reason for this distribution
2. Give two environmental variables that would need to be controlled to ensure reliable results.
3. (i) Suggest *two* different measurements that could be made in order to show the results of the experiment.
   (ii) Using *one* of these measurements, label the axes below to show how you would present the results of the experiment. State the units clearly.

4. Suggest *one* limitation of this experiment in relation to the plants in their natural habitat.

Books and journals

Read through relevant books and journals in the library. Supplementary A-level texts on more specialised subjects are worth browsing through. Of course, the first two volumes of this series are essential reading! Some journals that are targeted at school or introductory university level describe investigations that have been carried out – these can in turn suggest further ideas. Don't simply repeat them – think up a variation of your own.

The *School Science Review* and *The Journal of Biological Education* particularly carry sections on practical investigations.

I lifted a copy of the *School Science Review* off my shelf at random. It was volume 73, number 265, June 1992. In the Science notes on the contents page at the front I noticed an article titled 'Vacuum sampling of bark-dwelling arthropods'. In this article on page 90 the author Ian Kinchin describes the use of a battery-powered hand-held vacuum cleaner to suck up tiny arthropods that live in the crevices of the bark of trees. As he states, 'there is plenty of room for open-ended research', and he goes on to make some suggestions thus:

1. Compare the fauna living in the bark of different species of tree. It has been suggested that trees with rough bark will support more animals than those with smooth bark.

2. Investigate the possible zonation of animals in the bark at different heights above the ground and on different aspects of the trunk.

3. Investigate the relationship between the degree of epiphyte bark cover and the numbers of animals found.

4. Compare the number of animals found living on a lichen-covered tree trunk with that found on a lichen-covered wall.

Any of these would make an excellent investigation. They might trigger in your mind all sorts of other investigations of a similar nature but with, for example, different microhabitats.

Think of all the *School Science Reviews* there are, let alone all the other journals that are available. They should give you plenty of ideas.

Looking at another one – this time homing behaviour in the centipedes *Lithobius forficatus* (Linn) and *Lithobius variegatus* (Leach) by Lewis, Gliddon and Newbold, SSR March 1992, Volume 73 (264), pages 93–4. This article was written by the teacher and two former pupils of Taunton School in Somerset. Maybe your investigation will be worthy of publication!

If you wish to carry out a project on a particularly specific area then you should have a look through the appropriate journals. Read original papers that deal with the specific area in order to find out the sort of research that has been carried out.

Television programmes and newspapers

Keep an eye open for any possible interesting and appropriate programmes and articles. The scientific and nature programmes on TV, for example Attenborough's programmes, Horizon, Equinox, Tomorrow's World, etc. often suggest ideas for projects, but remember that many of these might be beyond what you need or are capable of – they might however be capable of modification and simplification.

There are many science journalists writing in the popular press. Read the papers with an open mind, looking for possible ideas. What is the evidence to back up any particular options? Perhaps you could supply further evidence in your investigation!

Always remember that you are not necessarily looking to repeat work that has been carried out, but rather you are hoping that what you see on TV or read in the papers might just trigger off a line of thought which will bear fruit.

Fieldwork

If fieldwork is part of your course this lends itself to endless ideas for projects. Generally there is only time for a superficial overview and many situations could be developed into more detailed studies. Keep your eyes open. Often data can be collected when you are on the course.

See the project on the gastropod *Nucella* in Chapter 7, which arose out of a fieldwork course.

Everyday life

Maybe you live on a farm. Do your parents work with living things, e.g. in horticulture? Discussion with parents on problem areas can be useful to them, particularly if there is an applied or economic aspect. There are plenty of ideas and problems in such areas that could be investigated.

I remember on one occasion discussing with a student what sort of a farm she lived on. She explained that it was a poultry farm, earning income mainly from egg production. On the farm were two large and identical poultry houses and together we came up with the idea of playing music to the hens to find if their egg production increased. Her father was of course pleased to find that it did and still plays music to them – what sort I don't know! This was a perfect situation for a controlled experiment since the birds came from the same breeding stock and the two houses were identical.

Hobbies and other interests

You might just have an interest in fishing, or sport, or collecting. Perhaps you keep tropical fish or interesting pets. Perhaps you play for a team and want to find out how fit the members are, or aren't! Maybe you have an interest in gardening, or growing vegetables, or even crossing varieties of flowers. What about weeds? You can readily adapt such interests to make investigation interesting.

Make notes of the various *general* areas that would be *possibles* for investigations. Try to select at this stage up to *ten* possible areas.

Then go through a process of elimination – removing those that would not be suitable for all sorts of reasons. Use the following check list to help your process of elimination, answering the questions as positive or negative for each of your tentative proposals.

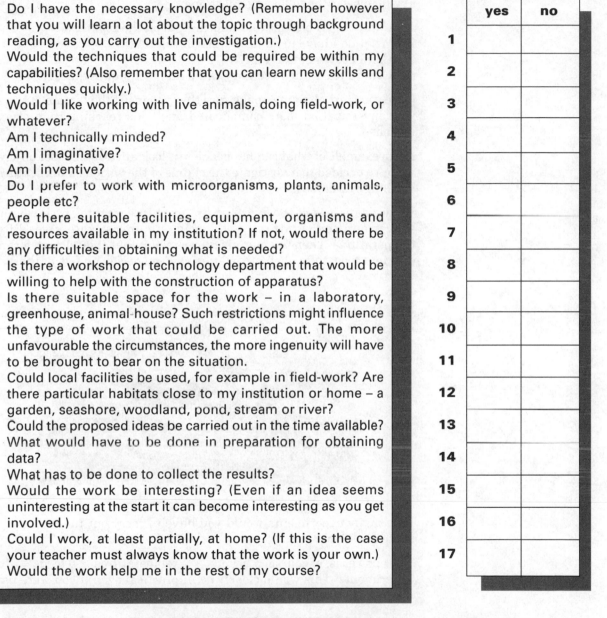

		yes	no
1	Do I have the necessary knowledge? (Remember however that you will learn a lot about the topic through background reading, as you carry out the investigation.)		
2	Would the techniques that could be required be within my capabilities? (Also remember that you can learn new skills and techniques quickly.)		
3	Would I like working with live animals, doing field-work, or whatever?		
4	Am I technically minded?		
5	Am I imaginative?		
6	Am I inventive?		
7	Do I prefer to work with microorganisms, plants, animals, people etc?		
8	Are there suitable facilities, equipment, organisms and resources available in my institution? If not, would there be any difficulties in obtaining what is needed?		
9	Is there a workshop or technology department that would be willing to help with the construction of apparatus?		
10	Is there suitable space for the work – in a laboratory, greenhouse, animal-house? Such restrictions might influence the type of work that could be carried out. The more unfavourable the circumstances, the more ingenuity will have to be brought to bear on the situation.		
11	Could local facilities be used, for example in field-work? Are there particular habitats close to my institution or home – a garden, seashore, woodland, pond, stream or river?		
12	Could the proposed ideas be carried out in the time available?		
13	What would have to be done in preparation for obtaining data?		
14	What has to be done to collect the results?		
15	Would the work be interesting? (Even if an idea seems uninteresting at the start it can become interesting as you get involved.)		
16	Could I work, at least partially, at home? (If this is the case your teacher must always know that the work is your own.)		
17	Would the work help me in the rest of my course?		

If you answer such questions honestly it should enable you to reduce your *possibles* list down to two or three *probables*. Think about these in more detail and at this stage approach your teacher(s) and discuss your proposals. Get as many opinions as possible because different people will have different approaches. They will advise you regarding the feasibility of your proposals and hopefully you should finally be able to come up with a firm topic for your investigation. Do not be put off if your favourite ideas don't work out. If none of the probables seem to be appropriate, try adapting some of the possibles.

5.3 KEEPING THE INVESTIGATION WITHIN BOUNDS

Once you have an idea it will generally be too wide in concept. The next stage is to refine your idea so that it becomes feasible both with respect to knowledge, techniques and time.

Try to answer the following questions:

1. Can I obtain background information on the topic easily?
2. What do I have to do to obtain relevant data?
3. Can I obtain data readily?
4. Could I learn the necessary skills and techniques quickly?

Once you start planning, make sure that you resist the temptation to make your investigation more complicated and wide reaching than originally intended.

As an example of what can happen, let us look at variables. Let us say that we have decided to investigate the claims of the various manufacturers of washing powders.

We decide to look at the five main brands. Since washing up is carried out at various temperatures you decide to investigate five different temperatures. Then the manufacturers claim that they 'digest' a range of different foodstuffs, dirt, etc – let us say you decide on five of these.

How many experiments would you have to carry out to find answers to these questions?

The answer is, of course, 5 brands $\times$ 5 temperatures $\times$ 5 foods = 5^3 = 125 experiments! This would clearly be impractical even if you were using a relatively simple technique for your tests.

The best way to estimate the number of experiments or tests that you have to carry out is to put the variables in the form of a grid.

Imagine the situation where there has been a report on television about more girls tending to take up smoking than boys. A student decided to investigate this in her own school. She decided to find out how many boys and girls in her school smoked at three different ages – 12, 14 and 16. There are three variables – gender, age and whether smoke or not. Gender has two elements – boys or girls; age in this case has three groups – 12, 14 and 16; and smoking consists of smokers and non-smokers. The student draws a grid to show these three variables.

	SECOND VARIABLE			
	1	2	3	THIRD VARIABLE
FIRST VARIABLE 1				1
				2
FIRST VARIABLE 2				3
				4

There are thus 12 boxes ($2 \times 3 \times 2$). This would be a manageable number of groups to test but it would depend on the number of people in each group. Say the student decided to test 10 in each group – that would mean testing 120 people (12×10). A lot of time would be required for this.

You have to balance the number of variables you wish to include with the number of experiments or tests you can carry out in the time available. *It is always better to keep the number of variables small and the number of replicates high* – your knowledge of statistics should tell you why. You must take the variability of living things into account.

5.4 PROCRASTINATION

It is particularly hard to get started and to keep going on an investigation. Procrastination (the art of putting things off until later) is the main obstacle to overcome.

Many of your short investigations will be part and parcel of your course, but a more extended investigation must not be left too long so that it cannot be completed and written up in time for final assessment. You always have to allow for setbacks, for rest assured, these will inevitably arise! You have no way of knowing what difficulties and hurdles lie ahead.

No doubt your teachers will assist you by setting deadlines when you have to submit your hypothesis, your plan, your raw data, your completed investigation in proof form, and your final completed work. Make sure that you adhere to these deadlines – they are not there as some form of punishment but to help you.

Once you get started you will find it easier to continue as you will become more and more interested in what you are doing, since it is uniquely yours.

5.5 THINKING THROUGH AN INVESTIGATION

This is the stage where you have to imagine that you are actually carrying out the investigation. Of course it will never turn out exactly as you imagined – but this is what makes it interesting, since you can compare what you thought and expected to happen with what actually happened. Everything in life is a bit like that – you plan continually but how many times do your plans turn out as you expected them to?

All investigations from relatively simple and straightforward guided discovery to more complicated open-ended investigations follow the same general pattern.

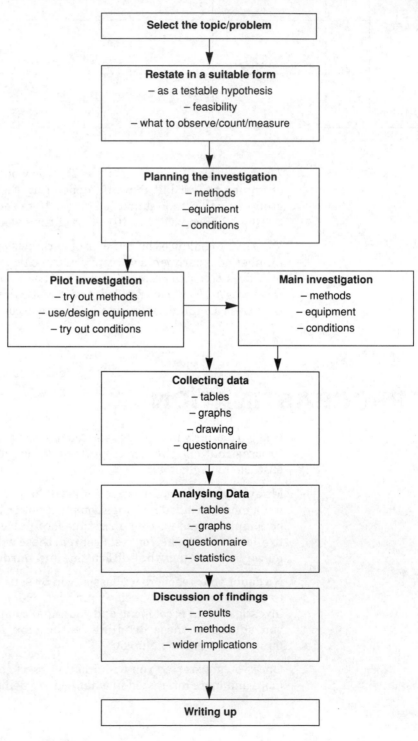

5.6 FORMULATING HYPOTHESES AND MAKING PREDICTIONS

Why do we need a hypothesis at all? It is in part psychological since it helps us to focus our minds. To design and carry out a good investigation and to consider the results requires quite a lot of mental effort, often for long periods of time. It focuses our energy and drive and helps us to plan properly. It tends also to encourage our sub-conscious mind to work away on the problems ('incubating') when we are doing other things. Without a hypothesis to provide this urge and to suggest what to observe and record we are likely to see nothing at all – it enables us to see things that we would otherwise not see.

How do we go from an idea to wording it as a hypothesis? Remember the lawn we were mentally mowing. Imagine it looked as if there were more daisies on the right-hand side of the lawn than on the left. Our hypothesis has to be stated in a way that it can be tested – it has to be in the form of a positive statement; it is a prediction, for example:

Hypothesis: There are more daisies on the right-hand side of the lawn than on the left-hand side.

Always remember that it doesn't matter if your hypothesis is actually correct or not. The important thing is that you can go on to find out if your hypothesis is correct or not. If it is correct, so far so good; if it is incorrect, you can then modify it or state in what way it is incorrect. You can then propose further more refined hypotheses and go on to test them (see Section 2.1).

This is what science is all about; it moves forward by testing hypotheses – if they are wrong the first time around, so what! They are improved and refined the next time around. The real importance of a hypothesis is the number of further hypotheses it generates – in the long run that is far more important than the initial correctness of the hypothesis.

So, do not be concerned that your hypothesis is right or wrong. You will not be penalised in any way if it is wrong. You may be so used to trying to get the 'right' answers to everything that you have become conditioned to think this way. Simply state the hypothesis in a way that it can be tested. If correctly stated the experiment becomes reasonably obvious.

The experiment should now be quite clear – in the example stated it will involve *comparing the numbers of daisies on each side of the lawn to find out if they are the same or not.*

Study plants or animals – note the conditions under which they do certain things – then make hypotheses as to which are the more important controlling factors in the complex of conditions, with a view to trying them out experimentally, or (more difficult) make hypotheses that can be tested in experiments as to the internal mechanisms.

Problems inevitably arise with what is called the 'null hypothesis'. Always remember that this is *not* your original hypothesis or idea that you are trying to test, but a statistical method which is used to find out if there is any difference between two sets of data or not, or if the data agrees to a prediction or not. In the example above concerning the daisies the null hypothesis would be that 'there is no difference between the number of daisies in the two areas' and we would find out if this 'null' hypothesis was supported or not.

If we use the null hypothesis then the results will tell us whether to reject or accept it – if we reject it, i.e. there is *not no difference* – then there must be a difference. If we accept the null hypothesis then we have to reject our experimental hypothesis. If our original hypothesis implies a difference between two groups, then it will be supported by *rejection* of the null hypothesis. If, on the other hand, the original hypothesis is a prediction, then it will be supported by *acceptance* of the null hypothesis.

This is all a bit crazy since we have come up originally with a positive hypothesis that there will be a difference and this is the whole point of the exercise. I just do not understand why this outdated way of doing things still lingers on in syllabuses – probably because the mathematicians say so and the poor biologists think that it must therefore be right!

The following questions were asked by students during lessons about flowering plant reproduction. They lend themselves to a wide variety of investigations.

Convert all of these questions into a form of a prediction that can be tested – as hypotheses.

1 Do larger flowers have larger pollen grains than smaller flowers?

2 Do wind-pollinated flowers make more pollen (as total mass) than insect-pollinated ones?

3 Do pollen grains need sugar to grow?

4 What does nectar contain?

5 Do all seeds store starch as a food store?

6 Do all plants store starch in their leaves?

7 Is the time it takes a seed to germinate related to its size?

8 Does freezing seeds for two or three days make them germinate quicker?

9 Does the time it takes seeds to germinate depend on how long they have been soaked beforehand?

10 Are tomato 'pips' more resistant to acid than apple 'pips'?

11 Does the dandelion 'clock' work?

12 Is the surface area/size of sycamore 'helicopters' related to the distance they can be dispersed?

Don't try to think what the right answer might be – we are not interested in answers at this stage – the investigations will give the answers. Here is the first one for you – remember that it has to be in a form that can be tested. It is quite straightforward:

(i) Larger flowers have larger pollen grains than smaller flowers.

Nothing could be easier. We can now design an investigation to find out if this hypothesis is correct, partially corrrect, or wrong.

5.7 PRINCIPLES

Before actually planning the investigation in detail you have to be clear about the principles on which it will be based.

Example 1

You have been studying the growth of yeast and you have been instructed to make up a culture medium containing sucrose. You wonder – does the growth of yeast depend on the type of sugar available? You think that this could make a good investigation. You convert your question into an appropriate hypothesis – the growth of yeast depends on the type of sugar available. Where do you go from here?

You have to ask yourself the following questions:

> 1 What type of investigation will I carry out?
> 2 What species of yeast will I use? What is readily available in the laboratory?
> 3 What sugars will I use, and in what concentration?
> 4 How will I make the yeast grow?
> 5 How will I measure the growth of the yeast?
> 6 How can I make sure that it is only the type of sugar that is affecting the growth of the yeast and not something else?
> 7 How many replicates have I time to carry out?
> 8 What sort of data do I want to obtain?
> 9 What would be the best way to present the data?
> 10 What statistical analysis could I use?

Let us look at each of these questions in turn and find out what sort of answers we could come up with.

1. Since I want to find out the effect of different sugars on the growth of the yeast the investigation will clearly be of the *experimental* type. I will grow the yeast under particular conditions.

2. The only readily available type of yeast is baker's yeast. I search through some books in the library and find that this is *Saccharomyces cerevisiae*. This should be suitable enough.

3. There is a range of sugars available in the preparation room – sucrose, glucose, fructose and maltose. These could be used. The concentrations of the various cultures will have to be the same. From looking up the literature I find that a usual concentration for culturing yeast is 20%. How is a 20% solution made up? This can be found from the literature.

4. From the lessons on the growth of yeast I discover that the growth follows an S curve and I must make sure that growth is at the maximum rate. I need therefore a starter culture from which I will take a given volume to add to each of my experimental culture solutions. This should not be too difficult.
   I must make sure that all quantities are the same and that all cultures are grown at the same temperature. I find out from looking up the literature that the optimum temperature for growth is 30°C and decide to use a water-bath (there are a number of these available) to maintain a constant temperature.

5. We carried out an experiment in class measuring the number of yeast cells using a haemocytometer. This could be used to measure the growth of the yeast over a period of time, sampling the cultures at particular time intervals. It also means that I will be using a constant

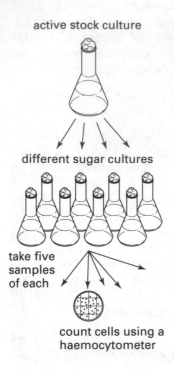

active stock culture

different sugar cultures

take five samples of each

count cells using a haemocytometer

volume of culture each time. I decide that this would be better than trying to measure the amount of CO_2 given off. I also know how to use the haemocytometer, how to count the cells properly, and my microscope technique is sufficiently good enough.

6. I must make sure that I use aseptic techniques so that unwanted organisms don't grow in the cultures. I decide to use conical flasks plugged with cotton wool – this should keep out unwanted organisms and let the CO_2 produced by the yeast escape. If everything else except the type of sugar is the same then I can be confident that any differences in growth will be due to the type of sugar.

7. Since I am going to use four different sugars I will need at least four cultures. Something could go wrong with them so I would be better to have two of each. If I take five samples from each at say ten different intervals I would have to count the cells in 100 samples. I have to count the cells in five squares each time under the microscope – a total of 500 counts! This seems a lot. I could, on the other hand, just leave the cultures for a given time and at the end of this period I could then count the cells. This would mean that I could take more samples from each culture to count. I must remember to swill the culture vessels to mix the cells thoroughly so that I take out a fair representation of cells. If there is good growth of the yeast I might have to dilute the sample in some way.

8. My data will consist of numbers of cells. If I take plenty of readings I should be able to end up with a mean and variance for each sugar substrate.

9. Since I don't have the time to take readings at various time intervals but just at the end of a given period of time, my results will be presented in tabular form and I could also present the overall data as a graph – a bar graph showing bars for each of the substrates.

10. Because I have obtained a mean and variance for each culture, I can use the *t* test to find out if there is any significant difference between them. I will make up a grid since I will have to carry out *t* tests on the data between each culture. I will need to carry out six *t* tests – sucrose *vs* glucose, sucrose *vs* fructose, sucrose *vs* maltose, glucose *vs* fructose, glucose *vs* maltose and fructose *vs* maltose. These results should give me some idea which is the best substrate for the growth of the yeast. The bar graph could show the means and confidence limits for each substrate after the given period of time.

Example 2

I was reading a hand-out from my biology teacher last night. It described how a company in Scotland genetically modifies sheep so that they produce human proteins in their milk. The gene for production of a particular human protein is injected into the pronuclei of fertilised sheep eggs. These eggs are then transferred to ewes, some of which in due course give birth to transgenic ewes. This is an efficient and relatively cheap way of producing such proteins since they can readily be extracted from the ewes' milk and can be administered to humans who cannot produce the proteins themselves. People who suffer from particular genetic disorders can thus receive treatment.

I wondered how people would react to using 'furry' bioreactors like sheep. I think that certain people get over-excited about mammals (rather than animals in general) simply because they are more closely related to us. How often do you hear of people being concerned with rare snakes or spiders, or even parasites? And as for plants! Are they concerned about a rare toadstool or a tiny alga? Maybe this would make the basis of a good investigation!

I need to ask myself the following questions:

1. What type of investigation will I carry out?

This is quite obvious since I want to find out about peoples' opinions. I will use questionnaires and/or interviews.

2. Who shall I ask?

I would like to compare the opinions of younger people with those of older people to find out if there are any differences – perhaps teenagers, those in their twenties, and those over twenty. I would also like to find out if vegetarians have different attitudes to transgenic animals than non-vegetarians. I will need to identify all these people so that they can be grouped accordingly – there will be six groups (vegetarians and non vegetarians in each of the three age groups). I will probably need at least 10 people for each group which means 60 in total.

3. What questions will I ask?

This will require considerable thought since I don't know much about transgenic animals and this will apply even more so to members of the general public. I will probably have to provide an information sheet for them to read first of all before responding to the questionnaire or interview.

I will have to ask questions about attitudes towards animals in general and then more specific ones in relation to the transgenic sheep. In particular I will have to think up questions that will test the idea that people are more concerned about mammals than other animals.

I will also need to carry out a pilot survey of the questionnaire or structured interview to find out if the questions are suitable.

4. How will I analyse the data that I obtain?

I could simply calculate the percentages of responses for each question for each group. However I would like to carry out appropriate statistical analyses to find out if there are any significant differences due to age or vegetarianism. I will need to find out which statistical tests would be suitable.

Now let us relate investigating to the lawn situation.

Experimental investigation

During our imagining about cutting the grass (see page 71) we wondered if cutting the grass caused it to grow more quickly. From our biology course we discovered that grass is a monocotyledon and the growing part is not at the tip but just above ground level, so that cutting the grass doesn't stop it growing – was this selection by grazers?

How could we state this idea as a testable hypothesis? Remember that it doesn't matter if it is right or wrong – we are only trying to predict what might happen. The hypothesis is therefore – *the more often grass is cut the faster it grows.*

How are we going to test this hypothesis? We could simulate what is happening outside by carrying out experiments in the greenhouse where we would have more control over the situation and where growing conditions would be more favourable. The grass could be grown from seed in trays and the grass could be cut with scissors.

What variables would we need to think about? Since all sorts of factors other than cutting could affect the growth of the grass – like light, temperature, humidity, pH of the soil, minerals in the soil plus those we couldn't know – we must make sure that they are controlled. Remember the Latin Squares (see page 51)? We could arrange the trays in that special way. How many trays should there be? There probably isn't very much space in the greenhouse and we would need a special table for the trays. We would need to fill all the trays with the same compost, water them all in the same way at the same time – maybe we could set up an automatic watering system.

Now we have to decide on a method to measure the growth of the grass. We could measure increases in height of the grass, or we could cut the grass from each tray and weigh it, but probably better still we could also dry the grass after cutting and then weigh it.

Let us say that we use ten trays, five of A which are going to be cut twice a week, say on Tuesdays and Fridays, and five of B to be cut once a fortnight on Fridays – so that at the end of two months we end up cutting both A and B at the same time. We could plant 20 seeds in each tray, all spaced in the same way.

We need to cut the grass in exactly the same way for each tray. We could set a ruler across the lips of the tray and trim the grass with the scissors level to it. All the cut pieces of grass from each tray are collected, dried and stored in plastic bags for weighing. Drying will have to be complete, i.e. there is no further decrease in weight. Some preliminary work will be required to find out exactly what procedures would be adopted.

We could store all the dried grass from the A and B trays and after two months compare the total weights of the cut grass and find if there was any difference. If the weight of the A grass turns out to be heavier than the B grass then the hypothesis would be supported; if the weight of the A grass is less than that of the B grass then the hypothesis would have to be rejected and a new hypothesis formulated; if both weights are the same then we could say that the frequency of cutting has no effect on the growth of the grass.

In our write up we could relate the findings to people cutting lawns, or to farmers cutting silage, etc. The results might just have important economic implications.

Observational investigation

Let us return to our daisies again and the cutting of the grass. You imagine cutting the grass, and the daisies, and suddenly you get the idea that cutting the grass might give the daisies an advantage since they might get more light. The next time you are on a grassy place you examine the daisies carefully and find that the leaves are down at the surface of the soil. If the grass was long then they wouldn't get much light. Your original idea seems more promising and possibly near the truth. You decide to investigate. Where can you start?

We predict by imagining an experiment, the results of which should enable us to decide whether our hypothesis is true or false. We tend however to persuade ourselves too easily that the results should be favourable to our hypothesis and we tend to design experiments that will produce results which support our hypotheses. Above all the experiment must be honest and give valid and reliable results. How could you find out if the daisies grew more when the grass was cut more often? At this stage you begin to think of an experiment which you could carry out.

How often should the grass be cut? It doesn't really matter. Let's say twice a week for the 'often' cut grass and once a fortnight for the 'rarely' cut grass. So the specified plots are cut either four times or once a fortnight.

How then are you going to measure the growth of the daisies? They could simply be counted. Perhaps you could simply compare the numbers of daisies in the 'often' cut plots with those in the 'rarely' cut plots. If there are significantly more in the 'often' cut plots then the hypothesis will stand up – if there is no significant difference then something is wrong with the hypothesis and you will have to modify it or come up with a new hypothesis. So a t test can be used to compare the mean number of daisies in the A plots (often cut) with the mean numbers in the B plots (rarely cut), but you need the variance as well (the standard deviation squared).

What variables need to be controlled? Think about dividing the lawn into two so that you can cut one half of the lawn often and the other half not so frequently. Then you think that other things might affect the growth of the daisies – the lawn has a slight slope so that the bottom of the lawn might be wetter than the top – the wetness of the soil might affect the growth of the daisies. Perhaps the lawn should be divided into four? Then again, there is a high hedge along one side of the plot which could shade the daisies so that it wouldn't make much difference if the grass was cut or not. The problem gets more and more complicated – maybe there is a difference in pH of the soil in different places, or different concentrations of minerals – how could the lawn be divided up so that all these and other factors would be taken into account? How many samples need to be taken? Can you find any information to help you? Look back to page 52.

You now have some idea how to go about the experiment, but need to order or sequence the steps that you have to take. You can either make up a list of the sequence of steps or draw a flow diagram. Here is a typical list.

1. Divide the lawn up into random plots (A and B plots).
2. Cut the A plots twice a week, always on Tuesdays and Saturdays.
3. Cut the B plots once a fortnight, always on a Saturday.
4. After two months sample the A and B plots and count the number of daisies in each plot.
5. Record the data.
6. Calculate the mean and variance of the counts from the A and B plots.
7. Carry out a t test.
8. Determine the level of p (given in the t table) to find out if there is any significant difference between the plots and if the daisies grew better in the 'often' cut grass plots.
9. Decide if the hypothesis is supported, requires modification, or is rejected.

Next you need to decide what apparatus and materials you will require. The lawnmower is available. You will need a quadrat frame. A tally counter would be useful for counting the daisies reliably. Check on the computer that a programme for the t test is available, or look up how to do a t test in your statistics book.

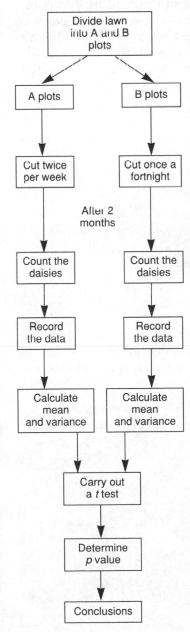

Divide lawn into A and B plots

A plots | B plots

Cut twice per week | Cut once a fortnight

After 2 months

Count the daisies | Count the daisies

Record the data | Record the data

Calculate mean and variance | Calculate mean and variance

Carry out a t test

Determine p value

Conclusions

Survey

We hypothesised that cutting the grass would cause an increase in the growth of daisies. To obtain evidence for or against this hypothesis we could design a questionnaire for people who have lawns. We could ask questions like: How often do you cut your grass during the summer – more than once a week, once a week or less than once a week? Are there daisies on your lawn – absent, rare, common or abundant?

Answers to such questions as these might highlight relationships which would help us to determine whether our hypothesis was correct or not.

5.8 EXERCISES IN THOUGHT EXPERIMENTS

EXERCISE 1

Imagine you have just been reading about acid rain and its effects in a biology book as preparation for an essay assignment. You have been wondering about an interesting and relevant topic for your individual study and think that there might be possibilities here. In discussions with your teacher the suggestion comes up that you could investigate the effect of acid rain on the rate of germination.

1
  i What will your hypothesis be?

  ii What organism will you use?

  iii What techniques will you employ?

  iv How will you carry out the investigation?

  v What type of data will be generated?

  vi What form of statistical analysis will you use?

EXERCISE 2

You have been studying genetics in a human biology course and have become very interested in the concept of population genetics and the Hardy-Weinberg equation. You would like to use your fellow students as subjects.

2
  i What are you trying to find out?

  ii What techniques would you use?

  iii How would you carry out the investigation?

  iv What type of data would be generated?

  v What analyses could you carry out?

EXERCISE 3

You are on a biology field course, and during a visit to a rocky seashore you find that the rocks are made of basalt and limestone. Attached to the rocks are large numbers of limpets (*Patella vulgata*). Your teacher informs you that the limpets are only attached to the rocks when exposed to the air, but that once the tide comes in, they move around scraping the algae off the rocks. Your teacher also explains that each limpet has a 'home' on the rock – always returning to the same place on the same rock when the tide goes out.

3   **i** What would your hypothesis be?

   ii What techniques would you use?

   iii How would you carry out this investigation?

   iv What sort of data would you be likely to obtain?

EXERCISE 4

In 1857 Pasteur observed that onion juice added to sugar solution prevented the development of yeast in it – he stated 'These facts justify the highest hopes for therapeutics'.

4   • Design an experiment to test this observation.

EXERCISE 5

For each of the following statements or questions (a) to (l):

5   • Propose a testable hypothesis.
   • Design an experiment to test your hypothesis, which should include:
   • a concise explanation of the principles on which your experiment would be based
   • an account of the procedures that you would use
   • possible sources of error
   • suggestions for suitable controls if applicable
   • an explanation of how you would present and analyse the results.

(a) It is thought that the transpiration rate of a green plant is related to the behaviour of the guard cells in the leaves.

(b) It has been found that different species of leeches vary in their oxygen consumption and it is thought that this determines their distribution in nature.

(c) The leaves of a potted plant have turned yellow.

(d) Can mice see colour?

(e) Freshly peeled potatoes turn brown quickly if exposed to the air. It is thought that this might be due to the presence of an enzyme.

(f) It has been found that in overcrowded conditions large tadpoles inhibit the growth of small ones. Is this due to competition for food or due to substances given out by the larger tadpoles?

(g) Some plants in the glasshouse failed to produce fruit although they flower satisfactorily there, and produce fruit when grown outside.

(h) It is thought that dissolved salts affect the respiratory rates in small aquatic insects.

(i) A species of beetle showed a preference for living under deposits of cow dung. It was assumed that this was because they used it for food.

(j) Insects with complete life histories usually metamorphose during the summer. Is the rate of metamorphosis affected by temperature?

(k) Since blow-fly larvae (maggots) are found mainly on meat and the adults are found on carbohydrates it was assumed that the main gut enzymes of the larvae would be proteases whereas those of the adults would be amylases.

(l) In some estuaries the tiny mollusc *Hydrobia ulvae* is found in very large numbers. It was thought that its distribution depended on the salinity of the water.

6 Writing the Report

The final stage of your project is the presentation of your investigation in the form of a report. After all the work that you have done you should put considerable time and effort into presenting it properly. The preparation of your report describing an intensive piece of personal investigative work offers considerable opportunities for the clear communication of the outcomes of such a study in as effective a manner as possible. Remember that your report may be the only evidence that the examiner possesses in order to make an assessment. A bad project will not be made better by a good presentation, but certainly a good project can be damaged by a poor report. Since the project report is the main evidence, like a scientific paper, that you carried out the work, it is only sensible that the evidence be presented in the best way possible.

Remember also that such writing is a skill increasingly required in most areas of work. Like other skills it can only be acquired by actually doing it – you can only become good at report writing by writing reports!

Unfortunately the writing up of the report is usually left to the last minute, so it is rushed in order to keep to a deadline. Try where possible to complete sections as you carry out the work, even in a rough state, so that you only have to tidy things up and complete some sections towards the end.

The following points, if observed, should help communication between you and the reader, rather than allowing the report to stand as a barrier. In many ways your report should resemble those found in scientific journals – it should be concise and conform to the style of a scientific paper, but remember the points mentioned earlier with respect to personalising your report (see page 64).

Most scientific papers follow a clear structure thus:

They begin with a short introduction to the problem, including references to earlier papers that relate to similar aspects of the problem. The writer then describes the materials and methods used in the work. Results are given in some detail, usually in tabular form. Often graphs are used to present the data. The significance of the work is then discussed and the paper closes with a brief summary of the conclusions and a list of references for the reader to look up if they so desire. Acknowledgement is also given to colleagues and others who have been particularly helpful.

The writing of a scientific paper, and of the report of an investigation, demands the same qualities as any other piece of prose writing. It calls for concise and accurate English and avoiding a stilted style. Ideally, scientific writing should be brief and to the point, but should not neglect conveying to the reader the atmosphere of the work and the thinking that went on behind the scene. Don't let freshness and originality be overcome by dull, scientific jargon. Remember however to maintain the rigour of good scientific work. It is the balance between these two that makes for good scientific writing.

The best way to do this is to imagine that you are telling someone else about your work and then to write it down just as you would tell it, in a sort of conversational style. Do not neglect humour if possible. Many humorous incidents, accidents (slight and not serious), puns and innumerable situations arise during the course of investigative work, which are never reported. Reference to the occasional one here and there can greatly lighten the load of the reader.

Always remember, it is more important to go for quality than quantity – length is not necessarily a virtue, and can usually put the reader off.

6.1 THE MAIN PRINCIPLES

Your report should basically cover

- what you wanted to find out
- how you found it out, and
- what you found.

and should indicate that you have acquired the skills of planning, researching, implementing, recording, interpreting, and concluding.

Planning

Identify clearly the situation to be investigated, which is stated as a testable hypothesis. Plan the investigation carefully and thoroughly, showing an understanding of the need for controls, replicates, sampling, etc. Risk assessments should be included.

Researching

Find out what has been written about the same or a similar situation by others. If, however, the investigation is original then not much will have been done by others – but there will be related information which will be important, for example, the application of particular techniques to the new situation.

Implementing

Carry out the investigation, particular experiments or surveys using appropriate techniques. Detail your methods, giving quantities, volumes, times, etc. Use appropriate SI units. Due regard to safety is essential.

Recording

Carefully record all your results, presenting them in an appropriate form, using tables, graphs, charts, etc.

Interpreting and concluding

Identify any trends in your results, and analyse your results using statistical tests where appropriate. Note any possible sources of error and limitations of the techniques used. From this analysis sound, logical conclusions can be drawn, and set in a wider biological context.

6.2 FORMAT

Your report can be hand-written, typed or word-processed. Since hand writing can often be difficult to read and typing can be difficult to correct, using a computer is best. Most institutions now have appropriate word-processing facilities and you should take the opportunity to learn how to use them. You will be likely to use computers no matter what you do in the future, whether in further education or at work, so the sooner you get into the way of using them the better.

With a computer it is easy to correct spelling or typographical mistakes, to edit what you have written and rearrange material using cut-and-paste techniques. A spellchecker program can be useful but don't rely on it and beware of technical terms. You may have a choice of fonts, but don't be tempted to use too many otherwise your report will look messy. Note in this book only two fonts are used (a 'serif' typeface for the main text and 'sans serif' for headings and diagrams).

There is a lot to think about before you start – line spacing, typesize, margins, style of headings, use of bold, italic and underlining, etc. These important points are illustrated on the next page. Chapter 7 also gives two examples of finished reports of investigations – you should get some ideas on presentation from these.

When you have printed off your pages, fasten them in a soft-backed file, with the title and your name written on the outside. Make two copies of your report – one for you and one for the department in your institution for future reference by students coming after you.

6.3   THE MAIN SECTIONS OF THE REPORT

Each investigation is of course unique, but all reports should contain the following sections:

Title – a snappy description of what your investigation is about.

Abstract – a short summary of your investigation.

Introduction – what you intend to do and why.

Hypothesis – your notion of the answer.

Background information – what you found from the work of others.

Materials and methods – what you needed to carry out the investigation and how you actually did it.

Results – what you found.

Presenting results – use of tables and/or graphs; statistics.

Discussion – your interpretation of the results and statement of the main findings.

Suggestions for further work – related investigations you would have liked to have tried, if you had the time.

Acknowledgements – who helped you.

References – details of references cited.

Appendixes – all the results you obtained and all the calculations you carried out. + plan + drafts, calculation of (screen prints) etc.

The finished report – some tips about good page layout

Use one side only of A4 paper (it will be easier to photocopy)

Number each page clearly

12 point typesize and 1½ line spacing is easy to read

Use bold type and underlining for emphasis, and italic for genus and species, book titles, etc.

Try to start main sections on a new page, or leave several lines space between sections

Use bold type for headings, larger type (e.g. 14 point) for main headings, and numbering for easy reference

If using a computer, justified type (i.e. each line is the same length) looks neater than having a ragged right-hand margin

Position headings and captions consistently (e.g. all ranged left)

Leave adequate space all round the text area, particularly the left-hand margin (to allow room for fixing in the file)

Layout of tables should be consistent and clear, using rules and evenly spaced columns (so they are easy to read)

Other pages may require diagrams – leave plenty of space for these, label them clearly and give each a figure number or caption

---

– 8 –

For one degree of freedom this value of χ^2 gives a p value <0.01. This result is highly significant, indicating that we can be very confident that the differences or similarities are not due to chance. In this case we can continue our investigation with larger samples, although the original hypothesis is amended to:

Immature *Nucella*, i.e. those of age 1 to 3 years, do not possess 'teeth', while mature *Nucella*, i.e. those over three years of age, do.

So the hypotheses to be tested in the main investigation are:

Hypothesis 1: *Nucella* from exposed areas have a higher incidence of 'teeth' than those from sheltered areas.

Hypothesis 2: Immature *Nucella* do not possess 'teeth', while mature forms do.

It is difficult to assess the relative importance of the environment in shell development against growth processes under genetic control. Further data might help to tell us more.

5 Main investigation

5.1 Selection of specimens

The same two coastal areas as those used in the preliminary work were selected. It was decided that 150 *Nucella* would be examined from each of the two areas. This represented a sizable population of *Nucella*, so in order not to damage them or upset the populations, counting of 'teeth' and opercular rings would have to take place *in situ*, and each *Nucella* set back after it had been examined from where it had been taken. Unfortunately the counting could not all take place on the same day. There were problems of the tide coming in, so that it took four days to collect the data.

Maps of the two areas drawn to scale were covered with acetate sheets containing superimposed grids of 1 m² squares drawn to the same scale. Each of the squares was numbered. Using computer generated random numbers within the range required, quadrats were identified for sampling. The random numbers were used to select coordinates of points at which to place a quadrat. These quadrat positions were then found on the shore and all the *Nucella* in each quadrat examined. This process was continued until the required number of 150 *Nucella* had been examined.

A table was drawn as follows to make recording of the data more straightforward and less likely to mix up the whelks. The table was filled in as each *Nucella* was examined, to minimise error.

5.2 Recording of data

Table 5.1

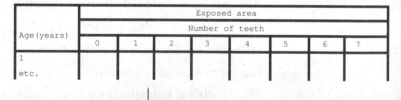

Age (years)	Exposed area							
	Number of teeth							
	0	1	2	3	4	5	6	7
1 etc.								

6.4 ORDER OF WRITING THE REPORT

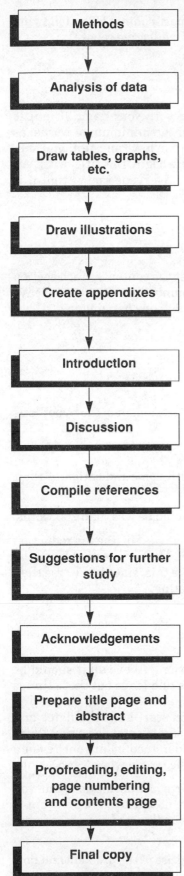

You will need more time and effort to write up your report than you think! You will always be under pressure to get your report finished in time. The answer is not to leave it to the last minute but to write it as you go along. These preliminary efforts can be hand-written, but it is better to get into the way of using the word-processor early on – you can key-in text and results, edit and improve as you go along, and generally save duplicating your efforts.

If you have kept a notebook detailing everything that you have done you should, at a reasonably early stage, have:

- a rough idea for a title
- a clear testable hypothesis
- details of how you carried out the work (including photographs if required)
- all the results that you have obtained
- your analysis of the results, including rough graphs, statistical test results, etc. (you may have print-outs of graphs if you used data-logging equipment or spreadsheets)
- a list of references.

As soon as you have completed the practical work you can therefore make a start to the following:

1. Describe in detail the methods you have used in carrying out your investigation.
2. Make up tables which summarise your results.
3. Make up tables summarising the results of your statistical analysis.
4. Draw any graphs carefully.
5. Draw any diagrams or other illustrations.
6. Create appendixes of your data and calculations.

You can then complete the other sections of your report:

7. Write the introduction.
8. Write the discussion.
9. Compile your reference list.
10. List your suggestions for further study.
11. Write the acknowledgements.
12. Prepare the title page and abstract.

Once you have reached this rough draft stage, let your teacher/supervisor have a look at it and take on board any suggestions that are offered.

Now proofread your manuscript, checking spellings (you can use a spell-checker facility but beware of scientific terms), typographical errors, grammar and syntax.

Once everything is sorted out and in order:

13. Number the pages.
14. Complete the contents page.

Finally, check through that everything is in order, and complete your prepared typed or word-processed script:

15. Print off two copies, collate the pages and bind neatly.

Then go and celebrate!

6.5 THE SECTIONS WITHIN THE REPORT

What exactly should each section in your report contain? The following general outlines should help you to produce an effective report.

6.5.1 Title

This is usually given on the cover page along with your name. The title should be brief and snappy and should tell, in the minimum of words, as much as possible about your investigation. You can have an additional sub-title giving more details if you wish. Do *not* begin the title with 'An Investigation into . . .', or 'To investigate . . .'. Everyone knows that it is an investigation into something!

6.5.2 Contents

The second page should repeat the title and list the contents. Each section and sub-section should be related to a page number. (Remember to leave this to the very end otherwise you will have to keep changing it.)

6.5.3 Abstract

This should summarise:

(a) the object of your investigation, including a statement of the hypothesis under consideration;
(b) the main methods used;
(c) the important results obtained;
(d) the major conclusions drawn together with some indication of their validity.

Keep the abstract short and to the point – it should be less than 200 words.

There is a tendency to write something like: '. . . in the Introduction section I introduce the investigation, and in the Methods section I give the methods used . . .'. Avoid stating the obvious like this, since it is worse than useless and starts your report off on a bad footing.

6.5.4 Introduction

It is always difficult to write a good introduction. Above all it should be relevant. Concentrate on the important issues and leave out those things which are not directly related to your investigation. A clear, concise and interesting beginning gets things off to a good start and stimulates and excites the reader. It should not, however, be a sort of extended essay. Write in a straightforward style which could be understood by anyone, even a non-scientist, by avoiding unnecessary scientific jargon wherever possible.

Try to resist the temptation to include all sorts of information that you gleaned when you were researching the topic, no matter how relevant it is. Long launches into personal glimpses of your thought processes is not what is required either.

The introduction should indicate clearly the nature of the problem and how you arrived at your particular study. Make sure however to avoid such statements as 'when I was considering what to do for my investigation my boyfriend/girlfriend/brother/sister/father/teacher/doctor/dentist, etc. said to me . . .' Nevertheless, if the idea actually arose during class discussion, or if your teacher gave you a list of titles to select from, then say so – be honest.

Any preliminary reading which directly led to the selection and identification of the problem should be given, with particular quotations where appropriate. References should be included concerning reports of similar work or previous experiments.

Explain as clearly as possibe the nature of your investigation and the hypothesis you tested. It is important to note that at this stage the hypothesis must only be given in a positive form which can be tested – there should be no mention at this stage of any null hypothesis, which should only appear (if at all) when you are carrying out statistical analyses (see pages 81–2).

In particular, mention any new approach, limitations and assumptions on which your work is based. Concentrate on those aspects of your investigation which are individual and unique to you.

6.5.5 Preliminary investigation

You can divide your methods into preliminary and main work, if that is what actually happened. Some projects because of their nature will not contain preliminary work, but they will be exceptions! The purpose of a pilot study should be to find out as much as possible about the organisms and methods you are going to use. Unforseen difficulties and other problems inevitably occur when carrying out an investigation – it is important to carry out preliminary tests to find out how the organisms will respond under the conditions proposed for the experiment.

Such questions as 'What is the level of variability?', 'What is the level of experimental error?', 'Will the proposed methods work?', 'Does the hypothesis require modification?', 'Will these questionaires provide the information that I am looking for?', are the sort that should be answered by the pilot study.

Sampling methods (if used) and controls must be carefully described and modified as necessary. Your techniques should at this stage also reveal the type of data and thus the type of statistical analyses you require. Give a short summary of the results, graphs and statistical analyses.

Finally, describe any modifications of your original experimental, sampling or observational methods, together with any modification to your original hypothesis.

6.5.6 Main investigation (Methods)

You should always describe your methods in sufficient enough detail so that if the investigation was repeated by someone else, with experience in the same field, similar data could be obtained. Concentrate particularly on any methods that are peculiar and individualistic, describing them in every detail.

Standard techniques and apparatus (that is, techniques that would normally be used during the practicals of biology courses) should not be described, but you should give a brief account of the principles on which your methods are based. Get a fellow student who knows nothing about the work to read over it, to find out if they could repeat the work exactly as you describe it.

If your project is ecological, describe in detail the habitats studied and where they can be found. Give precise details of the sampling techniques that you used. Experimental projects should contain precise descriptions of unusual apparatus, and details of any controls, replicates, etc.

You should also indicate, where appropriate, what precautions you took to ensure accuracy and safety.

All experiments should be dated. It is interesting to note that the date is probably more useful than any other single item of information in helping later research workers interpret experimental results in the light of further knowledge.

Answers to the following questions will help you to focus on those aspects of the work which are important:

1. What were the principles I used to design the investigation?
2. What equipment and apparatus did I use?
3. What materials did I use? How did I prepare them?
4. Did I use any new technique, modifications to an established technique, or a well-known technique in a new situation?
5. Did I change or modify my techniques in the light of experience from my preliminary work?
6. What controls did I use?
7. How many replicates/samples did I decide to carry out/take?

Drawings, diagrams and photographs

Illustrations such as drawings, diagrams and photographs can add greatly to the value of your report, particularly if the apparatus or methods you used were particularly individualistic or original.

Photographs, even relatively poor ones, are often better than a drawing because they are more likely to provide evidence that the work was personally carried out. If you are intending to use photographs these should be planned well in advance – take a number of shots of the same thing from different angles, different distances and under different lighting conditions. You can then select the best ones. A polaroid camera, if you can borrow one, is particularly useful since you can immediately see if you have captured what you intended. Black and white film is often better because you can develop it easily (with the help of the photographic society, if there is one) and make 'contact' prints as a cheap way of seeing what you have photographed before choosing the best shots to print to full size. Black and white prints are also better for photocopying than colour photographs.

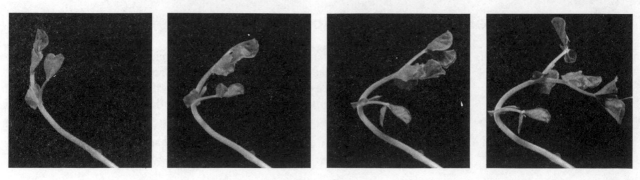

Drawings and diagrams are intended to be useful, not decorative, so you must ensure that they support your text and are easy to interpret. (See Volume 2, Chapter 2 'Drawing'). Here are some tips:

- Three-dimensional drawings look attractive, but 2-D is better for scientific diagrams.
- Write clear labels and space them so they are easy to read.
- Don't put arrowheads on leader lines – arrows suggest *direction*.
- Position labels so the leader lines don't cross over.
- Write full captions for each illustration, don't just code by number or letter.
- Position all illustrations immediately before, or at least as close as possible, to the text which refers to them.

Leave space on your draft script for finished illustrations. Try producing your graphs and diagrams on computer. You may be able to scan images, adjust them to the correct size and place them in the best position 'on screen' using a program such as Pagemaker.

6.5.7 Results

The presentation of results can cause difficulty, particularly when they are voluminous. Rather than include in the text several pages containing nothing but columns of figures, it is better to provide a summary and to put the complete data in an appendix – the flow of your account is therefore less likely to be interrupted. All raw data should be included somewhere in the report.

Clear distinctions should be made between observations (primary data) given in this section, and inferences (presented later).

Tables

Well-constructed tables can greatly improve a written report, getting lots of information across at a glance. Think carefully about the column headings, align numbers and put rules between groups of data so they are easy to read. (See Volume 1, Chapter 2 'Organising and Presenting Data', pages 6–11.) In every case a simple table summarising the results, usually containing means (with sample sizes), standard deviations and the results of statistical analyses, should be included.

Graphs

Think carefully about any graphs which you are proposing to include. There is a wide range of possible types for you to choose from (see Volume 1, page 11), but you need to choose the best type for your particular situation. Always aim for visual clarity, where the reader can see at a glance the relevance of the data. In particular, highlight any trends that you have identified.

You can draw your graphs on graph paper, laid out as you propose to have them in the final script. Include them in your hand-written submissions. If, however, you have produced the graphs by computer (either by data-logging or using a drawing programme), these can be printed out and stuck into a space left in the final report, or incorporated into Pagemaker.

Give explanatory captions and label the axes. Make sure that when the pages are put into the file that the labelling of the axes is not obscured. Keep the graphs and labels the right way up for ease of reading.

The following points should help you to draw effective graphs:

1. The size of the graph should be such that ample space is available for the margin, title, axis labels, scale numbers and key (where necessary). Remember to take the binding into account.
2. Single points on a line graph or scattergraph should be shown by means of a single dot, or a cross.
3. On a scattergraph, where the same point occurs more than once, the dot or cross should be surrounded by small circles of increasing diameter, one for each occurrence.
4. Shading, if used in histograms or bar charts, should be clear and unambiguous.
5. Graphs which need to be compared should, wherever possible, be drawn on the same grid, but the grid should not be cluttered up so that it is confusing. Try wherever possible to use confidence limits.

Note that, if your project consists of a series of experiments, it is usually better if the methods and results of each experiment are presented together. The 'results' section for each experiment would then consist of a summary table with any necessary discussion. The various strands can then be drawn together in the final discussion or conclusions section.

6.5.8 Evaluation of the results

Only when your results have been summarised and subjected to analyses does the most difficult part of the investigation begin – deciding what the data actually mean. Success depends, not so much on whether the results are 'right' or 'wrong', as on the systematic and honest approach taken, the reliability and validity of the results, and the conclusions reached. Was scientific rigour applied to the procedure? This is crucial to success!

Graphs can often be used to help with the analysis of data. Particular graphs can be used to identify trends, particularly the use of logarithmic and probability grids, and from these mathematical equations can be developed (see Volume 1, pages 50 and 61).

An understanding of statistics only really comes into its own when you analyse the results of your own work. In most cases it is difficult, if not impossible, to tell if your results support your hypothesis or not. It is only when you carry out the statistical analysis that this becomes clear.

Students are often horrified, distressed even, if they find that their investigation 'didn't work!' They feel that all their hard work has been wasted, and that they will be penalised because their original hypothesis turns out to be 'wrong'. Nothing could be further from the truth. An examiner or assessor would be very sceptical if they found that you got exactly the results that you expected. They are much more likely to be impressed by the honesty that your investigation is only really preliminary work – if you had been going on to study the topic further then you would have modified the hypothesis. Science moves forward – gradually refining or modifying hypotheses and thinking up new ones.

A suitable statistical test should be used to analyse the results, and to determine the significance level of any differences they show. Appropriate p values should be quoted and any relevant ones can be highlighted.

$p > 0.05$ (not significant)

$p < 0.05$ (significant)

$p < 0.01$ (highly significant)

$p < 0.001$ (very highly significant)

Students tend simply to give the p value together with a statement that the result is significant or not significant, and leave it at that. As such, this is relatively meaningless. You need to think carefully about the purpose of your investigation and what the p value actually means.

If you are comparing your observed results with predicted results then your original hypothesis (based on the idea that your prediction is correct) would be supported if there was no significant difference between them ($p > 0.05$) – in fact the *larger* the value of p the more closely the observations match the prediction!

If, on the other hand, you were comparing experimental with control results, your original hypothesis (based on the idea that the experimental group is different from the control group) would be supported by a significant difference between them – the *smaller* the value of p the more significant the difference. It is still not enough to say that there was a significant difference – you need to find out in what way the data were different. You need therefore to look back carefully at the data to make a statement about the significant difference – this can be done quite quickly by comparing means if using a t test, or observed and expected numbers if using a χ^2 test.

Remember, of course, the converse situations. If there is a significant difference ($p < 0.05$) between observed and predicted results, then the original hypothesis will have to be rejected or modified. If there is no significant difference ($p > 0.05$) between experimental and control groups, then we can question the efficacy of the experimental treatment.

Your interpretation therefore depends entirely on the type of investigation that you are carrying out, so you must be clear in your understanding. Note that I haven't even added the complication of a null hypothesis, which is actually not really required! (See pages 81–2.)

Hopefully the following table of p values will help you.

	$p > 0.05$ difference not significant	$p < 0.05$ difference significant
Observed *vs* predicted	SUPPORT	REJECT
Experimental *vs* control	REJECT	SUPPORT

Remember that relations between variates can *never* be proved – they can only be supported or disproved (in the sense that it is shown to be extremely improbable that they are true). Your analysis should be sufficient to show acceptance or rejection of the hypothesis under investigation.

6.5.9 Discussion

Your discussion should not just repeat the conclusions of the statistical analysis. It should be relatively comprehensive, considering the immediate findings of your investigation in a broader context.

Depending on the results of your graphical and statistical analysis, you might want to suggest improvements, refinements or modifications to your original hypothesis. You should also consider the wider significance of your investigation – how do your findings relate to your background reading, and how are they related to other findings of a similar nature? What is the biological significance of your results?

It is inevitable that unusual or anomalous observations turn up during any investigation. These should be carefully considered and their significance assessed in relation to the overall pattern of results.

It is also important to say something about how reliable and valid your results were.

Finally, round off with a summary of your findings.

6.5.10 Suggestions for further study

Science is a process and so scientific work is continuous and on-going. It is important to recognise that, owing to limitations of time, your work can only be a simple introduction – it is only a beginning, not the end, when you complete your investigation.

During the course of carrying out your investigation various ideas for further investigations will come to mind. You should list these since they form an invaluable bank of ideas for students following you. Also you probably found that if you had the opportunity to carry out your investigation again, you might do it quite differently – make suggestions. You could also mention any deficiencies that occurred owing to lack of time, facilities, etc. If you were carrying out your investigation again how would you do it differently?

Within an institution considerable expertise can thus be built up in particular areas over a period of years. For example, detailed on-going work in a particular local habitat can be carried out, as long as it does not interfere with or damage the habitat in any way.

6.5.11 Acknowledgements

All sources of information and advice should be given in this section. Do remember to preserve anonymity if it is required by particular examination or assessment arrangements.

Particularly mention all help given from outside your institution, and don't forget your colleagues and friends who can keep you going when things get tough and there appears to be no light at the end of the tunnel!

6.5.12 References (or Bibliography)

References should be quoted and listed in a systematic way. The Harvard system is usually used. This gives the author and year of publication in the text and the full reference in the Reference section or Bibliography, thus:

For a Book
Author, A.B. 1992. *Title of Book in Italics*. City of Publication, Publisher.

(followed by any particular comment about chapters or pages to which particular reference has been made).

For a Journal article
Author, C.D. 1990. Title of Paper, *Journal in Italics*, Volume, number, pages.

List the references in alphabetical order. If there is more than one reference for a particular author, put these in date order. If there are several authors for a reference, give the first two names and write '*et al*' to cover the remaining authors.

It should always be possible to trace a reference from the information given.

Examples
Garvin, J.W. 1995. *Skills in Advanced Biology, Volume 3. Investigating*. Cheltenham, Stanley Thornes.

Kitchin, I.M. 1992. Vacuum sampling of bark-dwelling arthropods, *School Science Review*, Volume 73, Number 265, page 90.

Toole, G. & Toole, S. 1995. *Understanding Biology for Advanced Level*. 3rd edition. Cheltenham, Stanley Thornes.

6.5.13 Appendixes

If you have lots of different sets of recorded data, label the appendixes APPENDIX A, APPENDIX B, etc.

These should be used for:

1. Bulky tables of raw data. It is not necessary to have all the data in the appendixes typed or word-processed, since this can be a very time-consuming process, but you may do so if you wish to make your report neat and complete. If you are going to require lots of the same sort of sheet, make up a master copy with appropriate headings to the table and photocopy them.
2. Detailed calculations of statistics should be given – this can be difficult to type or word-process, so you could write this out neatly if you wish.
3. Details of subsidiary experiments. Any unusual details of experiments that are not within the normal scope should be given in enough detail that they could be replicated.
4. Technical details of apparatus, equipment, etc. – particularly if they are unusual or have been constructed by yourself.

7 Examples of Investigations

So far you have been given lots of ideas and information on how to go about investigating. This chapter gives you two examples of reports based on projects actually carried out by past sixth-formers and produced for assessment. Look at their work critically and decide for yourself how well they set about their investigations, thought through their hypotheses, presented their findings, etc. Remember that not all the raw data is given in the appendixes.

7.1 AN OBSERVATIONAL INVESTIGATION

Tooth frequency in *Nucella lapillus*.

Contents

1. Abstract
2. Introduction and hypotheses
3. Background
4. Preliminary work
5. Main investigation
6. Results and analysis
7. Discussion
8. Suggestions for further study
9. References
10. Acknowledgements

Appendix

1 Abstract

This investigation attempted to discover why some *Nucella lapillus* (the dog whelk) possess projections or 'teeth' on the outer lip of the shell aperture. Two hypotheses were suggested – that *Nucella* develop 'teeth' when they become mature, and *Nucella* from exposed shores have a higher incidence of 'teeth' than those from sheltered shores because of the harsher environment of the exposed shore.

After carrying out preliminary work on 20 *Nucella* from exposed and sheltered coasts, and tentatively confirming the above hypotheses, larger samples of 150 *Nucella* were examined randomly from an exposed shore and the same number from a sheltered shore. The number of 'teeth' on each shell was counted and at the same time the age of each *Nucella* was determined by counting the rings on the operculum.

Statistical analyses indicated that there was a highly significant difference in the number of 'teeth' possessed by *Nucella* from exposed and sheltered areas – *Nucella* from exposed areas had more 'teeth'. Analysis of the age/'teeth' data indicated that young *Nucella* are less likely to possess 'teeth' than older *Nucella*. It would seem that the relationship between 'teeth' and exposed areas resulted from the greater percentage of mature *Nucella* found there. These answers lead to further questions which would be the subject of further investigations.

2 Introduction and hypotheses

While on a biology field trip to Portballintrae, we were examining the dog whelk *Nucella lapillus*, a carnivorous gastropod which was abundant all over the shore. I became more interested when, on closer examination, I noticed that some of them had tiny projections rather like teeth on the outer lip of the shell aperture, while others did not have them. Discussions with my fellow students and teachers did not help – nobody knew why some of the whelks had 'teeth' while others didn't, or what they might be for. I decided to find out as much as I could in the short time available.

I looked through what relevant literature I could find in the school library (see References). From this I found that mature and immature shells of *Nucella* differ – the outer lip of growing shells is thin and sharp whereas at maturity growth of the lip ceases and this region of the shell thickens, the outer lip becoming rounded, and it develops a series of 'teeth' along its inner edge. The whelks reach sexual maturity during the third year. This information was confirmed later by visiting a university library. There I came across a very useful book published by the Ray Society on *British Prosobranch Molluscs*.

I noticed, since studies on the field trip involved comparisons between sheltered and exposed regions of the rocky coast, that *Nucella* in exposed places seemed to have more 'teeth' than those from sheltered areas. Was there any connection? Did having 'teeth' help them to survive better in exposed areas? Were they able to grip the rocks better? On the other hand it seemed that *Nucella* develop 'teeth' on the shell when they mature, that is, during the third year.

Two hypotheses that could be tested were thus formulated:

Hypothesis 1: *Nucella* from exposed areas have a higher incidence of 'teeth' than those from sheltered areas.

Hypothesis 2: Only older *Nucella* possess 'teeth'.

3 Background

The classification of *Nucella* is (Eales 1952):

Phylum . . . . . Mollusca

Class . . . . . Gastropoda

Order . . . . . . Prosobranchiata (Streptoneura)

Family . . . . . Muricidae

Genus . . . . . . *Nucella (Purpura)*

Species . . . . . *lapillus*

The gastropod molluscs are a very large class containing one-shelled asymmetrical molluscs like the limpets and the winkles.

Nucella lapillus is commonly called the 'dog whelk'. Its shell is ovate with a pointed apex and consists of five to six inflated whorls separated by a fairly deep suture. The shell is basically a tube which expands from the apex (the blind end at the top) towards the bottom, the widest part terminating in the mouth of the shell, the peristome, from which the animal extends its head and foot.

The spiral of the shell is conical, each new and larger coil being added to the preceding one. This mollusc produces a yellowish-white to grey shell less than 35 mm long. The shell has a short spire with a large body whirl, an outer lip and a flared aperture (Barnes 1982).

In a young animal the edge of the aperture is sharp and fragile, the shell is thinner and the shell opening is larger than in a mature *Nucella*. When the animal, and thus the shell, stops growing, the edge of the mantle secretes a recurved lip (peristome). The outer margin is often toothed, and the aperture is oval. A thick lip indicates that the animal is an adult. There is a groove in the shell from which the siphon emerges.

The whole animal can withdraw inside the shell as required. When collected from the rock *Nucella* withdraws into its shell and closes the opening with a horny brown operculum.

Observations on *Nucella* show that several of them have a number of bumps or small projections along the outer lip of the aperture. These projections could be described as 'teeth', although they probably do not have any function in feeding. Only some *Nucella* possess 'teeth'.

Figures 3.1 *Nucella* without 'teeth'   Figure 3.2 *Nucella* with 'teeth'

Nucella that are going to produce 'teeth' cease to increase their shell length at sexual maturity. Instead of increasing their shell length the outer lip becomes thicker and 'teeth' emerge. Therefore, the outer lip thickening and protruding 'teeth' decrease the size of the aperture (Yonge 1958).

Nucella usually aggregate in comparatively sheltered hollows on the middle shore up to the sub-littoral zone (Barnes 1982). In these regions barnacles and mussels are preyed upon by this carnivorous gastropod. It is capable of boring a small hole in the shell of its prey using its proboscis and enzymes to get at the food inside.

Figure 3.3 *Nucella* feeding on a limpet

Nucella is the main predator of intertidal barnacles. It can be a pest of commercial mussel and cockle beds.

Nucella has separate sexes. They congregate in rock crevices in winter and spring. After pairing the female lays 6 to 31 yellow flask-shaped capsules on the rock. Each capsule contains several hundred eggs, but only a few of these are fertile. The fertile eggs develop inside the capsules, feeding on the infertile eggs.

Nucella is widely distributed on the European coast of the Atlantic and is one of the commonest molluscs of British waters. To survive exposure to strong waves, *Nucella* stop moving around and pull their shells closer to the rock surface. They occur wherever there are rocks which are not too exposed, and on rough shores where they can shelter from the waves in rock crevices.

Growth of *Nucella* depends on the quantity of suitable food available and on their age. Periods of growth, followed by intervals where no growth takes place, results in ridges or lines of growth around the shell. Whenever food is scarce or conditions bad, only a small amount will be added to the shell. During favourable conditions a band of new shell will be added. The shell is therefore a record of the molluscs' past life. Its good and bad years can be determined from the pattern of lines of growth on the shell. The colour of the shell can be influenced by the animal's diet – if it feeds on mussels then there are often dark brown growth lines on the shell.

4 Preliminary work

Exposed and sheltered areas were selected. The sheltered area was the west side of Portballintrae Bay while the exposed area is further out to sea – indeed it is the high rocks of the exposed area that provide shelter from the winds to the sheltered area.

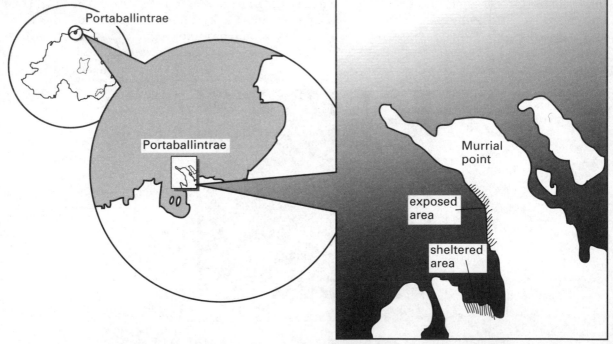

Figure 4.1 Map to show sheltered and exposed areas.

Twenty *Nucella* were collected at random from both exposed and sheltered areas – simply by walking along and picking them up. When samples are used to make inferences about a population, it is important that the individuals selected are a fair representation of the population. The samples should always be free from bias. The samples were examined where they were picked up. Data was entered in predrawn tables which indicated the number of teeth on each *Nucella* – this was quite straightforward, and the teeth are easy to count. The results were summarised as follows:

Table 4.1

Number of 'teeth'	Frequency from sheltered area	Frequency from exposed area
0	11	6
1	0	0
2	1	0
3	2	2
4	1	1
5	5	7
6	0	2
7	0	2

The data was then summarised from the two areas for simple statistical analysis:

Table 4.2

	Exposed area	Sheltered area
Nucella with 'teeth'	14	9
Nucella without 'teeth'	6	11

A χ^2 2 × 2 contingency test was carried out on these data (Garvin 1986, page 104) as follows:

Table 4.3

		Type of shore		Row totals
		Exposed	Sheltered	
Type of *Nucella*	with 'teeth'	14 (11.5)	9 (11.5)	23
	without 'teeth'	6 (8.5)	11 (8.5)	17
Column totals		20	20	40

From this table of observed and expected (in brackets) figures we can see that there are more with 'teeth' from the exposed coast than would be expected by chance (14 compared to 11.5), and fewer without 'teeth' (6 compared to 8.5). On the other hand, in the sheltered area those with 'teeth' are less than expected by chance (9 compared to 11.5), and there are more without 'teeth' (11 compared to 8.5). Are these differences significant?

A χ^2 test of these data gives a value of 1.638. Looking up the table of χ^2 we find that this corresponds to a *p* value of greater than 0.05 – the differences are therefore not significant; in other words, any differences that were found were due to chance. In this pilot sample only small numbers were examined – the results could be significant if larger numbers were used.

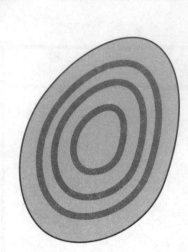

Figure 4.2 Diagram of the operculum – this *Nucella* is four years old

In the light of the preliminary work it would seem that perservering with the original hypotheses, *viz* that *Nucella* from the exposed area have more 'teeth' than *Nucella* from the sheltered area, is acceptable.

The background reading suggested that the 'teeth' might be due to the age of *Nucella*. It is important therefore to take the age of the *Nucella* into account. Do the 'teeth' develop as *Nucella* get older?

A simple way of finding the age of many molluscs is to examine the operculum, a tough leathery oval plate that closes off the aperture of the shell. This can be done with *Nucella* using a simple hand-lens. Rings are found on the operculum rather like tree rings, each lighter-coloured area between the rings representing growth during the spring and summer.

The same samples of 20 *Nucella* from the exposed area and 20 from the sheltered area were examined and their ages determined. As the age of each one was recorded so also were the number of teeth. The results were as follows:

Table 4.4

Exposed area		Sheltered area	
Age in years	Number of 'teeth'	Age in years	Number of 'teeth'
5	7	4	5
4	5	4	3
5	5	3	0
2	0	4	5
4	5	4	0
5	5	2	0
4	4	2	0
5	0	5	0
6	6	5	5
3	0	4	0
5	5	3	0
5	5	5	0
4	0	6	0
4	3	3	0
4	3	4	3
5	6	4	5
5	5	5	0
3	0	3	4
4	0	5	5
4	7	4	2

From these figures there doesn't seem to be much sense. There doesn't appear to be any connection between age and the number of teeth.

By grouping the age data into immature *Nucella* (age up to and including three years) and mature *Nucella* (age above three years) we can perhaps get a clearer picture.

These data were entered in a 2 x 2 contingency table thus:

Table 4.5

	Nucella without 'teeth'	*Nucella* with 'teeth'	Totals
Immature *Nucella* (1–3 years)	8	1	9
Mature *Nucella* (>3 years)	9	22	31
Totals	17	23	**40**

Expected figures were calculated. These are shown in brackets in the following table:

Table 4.6

	Nucella without 'teeth'	*Nucella* with 'teeth'	Totals
Immature *Nucella* (1–3 years)	8 (3.825)	1 (5.175)	9
Mature *Nucella* (>3 years)	9 (13.175)	22 (17.825)	31
Totals	17	23	**40**

Examination of these arranged data show that there are more immature *Nucella* without 'teeth' than one would expect by chance alone (8 as against 3.825) and fewer mature *Nucella* without 'teeth' than one would expect (9 against 13.175). All the *Nucella* with 'teeth' were mature except one.

Calculation of χ^2 (using Yates' correction factor since there is only one degree of freedom) gives:

Table 4.7

O	E	(O-E)	(O-E)-0.5	$[(O-E)-0.5]^2$	$[(O-E)-0.5]^2/E$
8	3.825	4.175	3.675	13.5	3.53
1	5.175	4.175	3.675	13.5	2.61
9	13.175	4.175	3.675	13.5	1.02
22	17.825	4.175	3.675	13.5	0.76

$$\chi^2 = 7.92$$

For one degree of freedom this value of χ^2 gives a p value <0.01. This result is highly significant, indicating that we can be very confident that the differences or similarities are not due to chance. In this case we can continue our investigation with larger samples, although the original hypothesis is amended to:

Immature *Nucella*, i.e. those of age 1 to 3 years, do not possess 'teeth', while mature *Nucella,* i.e. those over three years of age, do.

So the hypotheses to be tested in the main investigation are:

Hypothesis 1: *Nucella* from exposed areas have a higher incidence of 'teeth' than those from sheltered areas.

Hypothesis 2: Immature *Nucella* do not possess 'teeth', while mature forms do.

It is difficult to assess the relative importance of the environment in shell development against growth processes under genetic control. Further data might help to tell us more.

5   Main investigation

5.1 Selection of specimens

The same two coastal areas as those used in the preliminary work were selected. It was decided that 150 *Nucella* would be examined from each of the two areas. This represented a sizable population of *Nucella*, so in order not to damage them or upset the populations, counting of 'teeth' and opercular rings would have to take place *in situ*, and each *Nucella* set back after it had been examined from where it had been taken. Unfortunately the counting could not all take place on the same day. There were problems of the tide coming in, so that it took four days to collect the data.

Maps of the two areas drawn to scale were covered with acetate sheets containing superimposed grids of $1\,m^2$ squares drawn to the same scale. Each of the squares was numbered. Using computer generated random numbers within the range required, quadrats were identified for sampling. The random numbers were used to select coordinates of points at which to place a quadrat. These quadrat positions were then found on the shore and all the *Nucella* in each quadrat examined. This process was continued until the required number of 150 *Nucella* had been examined.

A table was drawn as follows to make recording of the data more straightforward and less likely to mix up the whelks. The table was filled in as each *Nucella* was examined, to minimise error.

5.2 Recording of data

Table 5.1

Age (years)	Exposed area							
	Number of teeth							
	0	1	2	3	4	5	6	7
1 etc.								

The completed tables for both areas are given in the Appendix.

5.3 Analysis of data

First of all a 2 × 2 contingency table was prepared to tally the *Nucella* from the exposed and sheltered areas that had 'teeth' and those that hadn't, like that used in the preliminary work. The summary of the observed numbers were as follows:

Table 5.2

		Type of shore		Row totals
		Exposed	Sheltered	
Type of *Nucella*	with 'teeth'	125	76	201
	without 'teeth'	25	74	99
Column totals		150	150	**300**

The numbers expected due to chance alone were calculated so that a χ^2 analysis could be carried out. The expected numbers are given in brackets.

Table 5.3

		Type of shore		Row totals
		Exposed	Sheltered	
Type of *Nucella*	with 'teeth'	125 (100.5)	76 (100.5)	201
	without 'teeth'	25 (49.5)	74 (49.5)	99
Column totals		150	150	**300**

Table 5.4

O	E	(O–E)	(O–E)–0.5	$[(O-E)-0.5]^2$	$[(O-E)-0.5]^2/E$
125	100.5	24.5	24	576	5.73
1	100.5	24.5	24	576	5.73
9	49.5	24.5	24	576	11.64
22	49.5	24.5	24	576	11.64

$$\chi^2 = 34.74$$

This gives a χ^2 value of 34.74. With one degree of freedom this represents a *p* value of <0.001. The result is very highly significant, meaning that the presence of 'teeth' is not due to chance but to some other factor, presumably in this case the type of coast.

Next the data concerning the age of the *Nucella* and the possession of 'teeth' was considered. The raw data was grouped as follows:

Table 5.5

| Type of *Nucella* | | Age of *Nucella* | | Row totals |
		Immature (1–3)	Mature (>3)	
Type of *Nucella*	with 'teeth'	7	194	201
	without 'teeth'	26	73	99
Column totals		33	267	**300**

Expected numbers were calculated and entered in the table thus:

Table 5.6

| Type of *Nucella* | | Age of *Nucella* | | Row totals |
		Immature (1–3)	Mature (>3)	
Type of *Nucella*	with 'teeth'	7 (22.1)	194 (178.9)	201
	without 'teeth'	26 (10.9)	73 (88.1)	99
Column totals		33	267	**300**

From these figures χ^2 was then calculated:

Table 5.7

O	E	(O-E)	(O-E)-0.5	$[(O-E)-0.5]^2$	$[(O-E)-0.5]^2/E$
7	22.1	15.1	14.6	213.16	9.65
194	178.9	15.1	14.6	213.16	1.19
26	10.9	15.1	14.6	213.16	19.55
73	88.1	15.1	14.6	213.16	2.42

$$\chi^2 = 32.81$$
$$df = 1$$
$$p < 0.001$$

This result is very highly significant. The presence of 'teeth' is linked to the maturity of the *Nucella*.

7 Discussion

Why do more *Nucella* in exposed areas have 'teeth' than *Nucella* in sheltered areas? If we look at the analysed data in the tables we find that at one to three years old a small minority of *Nucella* possessed 'teeth', whereas at more than three years the majority of *Nucella* possessed 'teeth'. This backed up the assertion that only mature *Nucella* possess teeth, and that maturity develops during the third year. *Nucella* reach sexual maturity at four years old (Yonge 1958).

Thickening the outer lip and producing 'teeth' makes the aperture narrower. This would be a good deterrent to the shore crab, making it difficult for it to thrust its claw into the aperture to pull out the mollusc within.

I observed that 'tooth' formation significantly increased beyond three years.

I still have not been able, from the information obtained, to explain satisfactorily the function of the 'teeth'.

8 Suggestions for further study

1. Repetition of this investigation on coasts of different levels of exposure.

2. Finding answers to suggestions that the 'teeth':

   (a) help the *Nucella* to 'hang on' to the rocks

   (b) prevent crabs from pulling them out of their shells.

9 References

Angel, H. *The Guinness Book of Seashore Life*. Guinness Superlatives Ltd. Enfield (1981).

Barker, P. *Life in the Aquarium*. G.Bell and Sons Ltd. London (1960).

Barnes, R. *Coasts and Estuaries*. Book Club Associates, London (1982).

Barrett, J. and Yonge, C.M. *Collins Pocket Guide to the Sea Shore*. Collins, London (1958 – reprinted 1984).

Eales, N.B. *The Littoral Fauna of Great Britain*. Cambridge University Press. London (1939 – reprinted 1952).

Fretter,V. and Graham, A. *British Prosobranch Molluscs*. The Ray Society, London (1962).

Garvin, J.W. *Skills in Advanced Biology, Vol.1 – Dealing with Data*. Stanley Thornes Ltd. Cheltenham (1986).

Yonge, C.M. *The Sea Shore*. Collins, London (1958).

10 Acknowledgements

I would like to thank my teachers for taking time to guide me when I needed it, and the staff of Queen's University Science Library who were more than helpful.

Appendix

Ages and number of 'teeth' of *Nucella* from the **exposed coast** – raw data:

Age/years	5	4	5	2	4	5	4	5	6	3	5	5	4	4	4	5	5	3	4	4
No.of 'teeth'	7	5	5	0	5	5	4	0	6	0	5	5	0	3	3	6	5	0	0	7

Ages and number of 'teeth' of *Nucella* from the **sheltered coast** – raw data:

Age/years	4	4	3	4	4	2	2	5	5	4	3	5	6	3	4	4	5	3	5	4
No. of 'teeth'	5	3	0	5	0	0	0	0	5	0	0	0	0	0	3	5	0	4	5	2

Summary of ages and number of 'teeth' of *Nucella* from an **exposed coast**:

Exposed area								
	Number of 'teeth'							
Age (years)	0	1	2	3	4	5	6	7
1								
2	1							
3	4					1		
4	12	1		3	2	21	13	4
5	8			2	2	32	20	6
6						5	13	

Summary of the number of 'teeth' of *Nucella* from a **sheltered coast**:

Sheltered area								
	Number of 'teeth'							
Age (years)	0	1	2	3	4	5	6	7
1								
2	4					1		
3	17				1	2		
4	31	1	2	6	8	18	1	
5	21		1	1	2	15	6	
6	2	1			2	4	2	
7						1		

7.2 AN EXPERIMENTAL INVESTIGATION

A COMPARISON OF KINESTHETIC SENSITIVITY BETWEEN MUSICIANS AND NON-MUSICIANS

CONTENTS

INTRODUCTION

The five physical senses are normally divided into sight, smell, taste, touch and hearing. The kinesthetic sense is a sub-division of the sense of touch. It is the kinesthetic sense which makes us aware of the location of the different parts of our bodies in relation to space and to each other, even when blindfolded; it also makes us aware of the speed and direction of any movement of the head or limbs.

In the following investigation I have attempted to find out if there is a relationship between a high degree of training in playing a musical instrument and development of the kinesthetic sense.

I have chosen to study kinesthetic ability for my investigation because I am studying music at A-level and as far as I know, very little work has been done in this area.

BACKGROUND INFORMATION

'Kinesthesis' means 'sensitivity to movement' and hence the kinesthetic sense refers to our awareness, even with our eyes closed, of posture, the location of the body and its parts in space, and their orientation with respect to gravity.

Kinesthesis is of two types:

(a) vestibular kinesthesis – this makes us sensitive to the speed and direction of movements of the head, and

(b) touch kinesthesis – which makes us aware of the speed and direction of movements of the limbs.

It is the latter which forms the field of investigation in this project.

The nervous system

The mammalian nervous system consists of a central nervous system (CNS), a concentrated mass of interconnected nerve cells, and the peripheral nerves which link the CNA with the body's receptors and effectors. There are two components of the nervous system – the autonomic system for the control of internal organs, and the somatic system which carries messages to the CNS from sense organs, muscles and joints, and from the CNS to the sense organs and muscles.

Receptors in the joints are sensitive to the precise angle at which joints are bent, and stretch receptors in the muscles are sensitive to how much the muscle is contracted – such information indicates to us the amount of movement and position of a limb. Such receptors are known as proprioceptors.

The part of the brain responsible for kinesthetic control is the cerebellum. It is situated just anterior to the medulla and comprises a greatly folded expansion of the hindbrain. It has been found that removal of the cerebellum from an animal makes it unbalanced and leaves it incapable of making accurate voluntary movements. Naturally occurring cerebellar disorders are particularly debilitating because of the lack of balance and muscular coordination, with resulting severe clumsiness.

Sensorimotor skills

As the term suggests, sensorimotor skills involve a close relationship between sensation and movement. Proficiency in a wide range of activities, ranging from writing, driving, typing and playing a musical instrument, are dependent upon one's ability to move limbs or parts of limbs accurately and within specified time limits. Sensorimotor skills take a long time to develop and require a high level of fine muscular coordination and manual dexterity, i.e. they are dependent on the efficient functioning of the kinesthetic sense.

SELECTION OF A LIMITED TOPIC FOR PRACTICAL INVESTIGATION

Since little is known about the kinesthetic sense I wasn't sure where to start. I was advised to keep the investigation relatively simple so that I could control most variables and draw reasonably valid conclusions from my results.

I wondered if the kinesthetic sense would be more highly developed in people who were proficient in a sensorimotor skill which required a greater than normal manual dexterity and precision.

An example of such a skill is the ability to play a musical instrument, and since I have this ability and am studying music for A-level, the investigation of kinesthetic ability in relation to musicians and non-musicians interested me considerably.

PROBLEMS IN THE AREA OF INTEREST

In order to carry out an experiment on musicians and non-musicians it was first of all necessary to decide on a system of classifying individuals into either one group or the other.

I carried out a survey among the music teachers and their students in order to find out the period of time necessary for students to develop the skill of playing, to the extent of being able to 'sight-read' (that is, without first having to 'look for' the position of the notes) and to move accurately from one position on the instrument to another.

A period of two years was decided as being the average time necessary to reach this standard.

The following system of classification was devised.

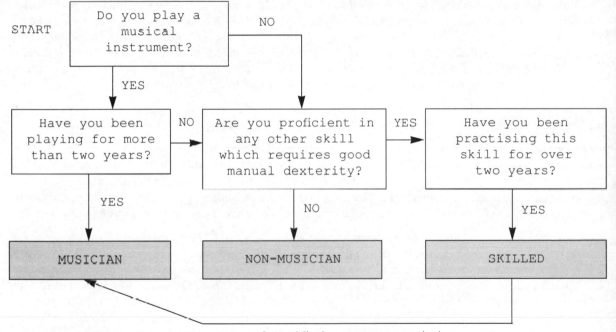

classified same as musician

Assuming that two years is the approximate time required to reach a reasonable level of proficiency in any highly developed sensorimotor skill, and that musicianship is representative of such skills, the question of whether the individual had any other skill was introduced so that other variables that could influence the outcomes could be controlled. Good typists, for example, can perform a highly developed sensorimotor skill, requiring greater than normal coordination and manual dexterity, and so these individuals could not be classified as non-musicians who have no 'highly developed' sensorimotor skill.

Definition of the hypothesis

In order to play fluently, musicians must know the distance between notes and be able to change this distance very quickly and accurately in order to change the notes. The layperson or novice finds this very difficult to do, so it would seem to be a reasonable suggestion that musicians would be better at sensing small changes in distance between the fingers (as a measure of kinesthetic ability) than non-musicians.

Hypothesis

Musicians have greater kinesthetic ability than non-musicians.

PLANNING OF THE PROCEDURE

1 Design of apparatus to test kinesthetic ability

The simplest apparatus which I could devise for my experiments consisted of a series of small wooden blocks – one to act as a standard, and four of slightly different lengths, all suitable for being held comfortably between the thumb and middle finger.

A suitable length for the standard block had to be determined. The subject was asked to shake one hand vigorously until it was totally relaxed, and to let it down loosely. I then measured the distance between the tip of the thumb and the tip of the middle finger while the hand was in this position. I am assuming that when the hand is relaxed there is minimum tension in the muscles and joints and that this must be the most natural and comfortable position for the fingers. In a group of 30 subjects, chosen at random, this mean distance was 6 cm – so this was the length of the standard block.

To determine suitable lengths for the other blocks, several blocks of different sizes were made and tested on 30 students, chosen at random.

Each subject was instructed to hold the standard block for 10 seconds. This was then set down and the second block picked up and held for 10 seconds. The subject then had to say if the second block felt longer, shorter, or the same length as the standard. The standard block was returned to the subject for a further 10 seconds and the procedure repeated, using a different second block.

Results showed that 100% of the individuals tested were able to detect either an increase or a decrease of 7 mm in the length of the block. However, with an increase or decrease of 5 mm, not all of the individuals tested gave the correct answer. With a difference of 2 mm almost 50% of the individuals gave the incorrect response. 2 mm had to be my minimum difference because it was the smallest degree by which I could accurately vary the length of the blocks.

From these results I decided that variations of 5 mm and 2 mm from the length of the standard would be suitable for my test blocks.

The blocks were constructed from mahogany because hard wood permits more accurate shaping than soft wood. The blocks were cut to approximately the correct lengths and then adjusted to the exact length using fine sand-paper. All other dimensions were kept constant. The finished blocks, for convenience called A, B, C, D and E, had the following dimensions:

$$A = 2 \times 2 \times 6.5 \text{ cm}$$
$$B = 2 \times 2 \times 6.2 \text{ cm}$$
$$C = 2 \times 2 \times 6.0 \text{ cm (the standard)}$$
$$D = 2 \times 2 \times 5.8 \text{ cm}$$
$$E = 2 \times 2 \times 5.5 \text{ cm}$$

'Congratulations'

.... Dylan Manickum ....

Well done for all your hard work and good manners.

You have won a place on the Jewel Celebration for all Milton house members on

Thursday afternoon in school

You will be entertained by Tazz.

You may bring a change of clothes if you would like the get changed for the celebration.

2 Selection of subject sample

Since kinesthetic ability could change with age, it was necessary for me to have a population in which age was as consistent as possible. Being a member of the sixth form, where all the students were either 17 or 18 years of age, I decided to carry out my experiments on sixth formers. It was also possible that this would also reduce the effect of other unknown variables.

I took down the names of all the students in the sixth form from the class lists. I then classified them as musicians or non-musicians by asking each student the questions, in the order shown by the flow diagram.

Unfortunately this survey indicated a shortage of students with the ability to play a musical instrument and so I expanded my population by taking in the names of 17 and 18 year old students from the membership lists of the County Youth Orchestra of which I am a member.

I then gave each name on the musician and non-musician lists a number, and by using random numbers generated on the computer, I selected names until I had 50 musicians and 50 non-musicians.

METHODOLOGY AND RESULTS

Method

1. The subjects were blindfolded and asked to extend their right hand (if right-handed), or their left hand (if left-handed).

2. The standard block was then placed in the subject's hand and they were instructed to hold it between the tip of the thumb and the tip of the middle finger.

3. After 10 seconds the block was removed and the subjects asked to relax their hand and flex their fingers, thus avoiding the temptation to 'fix' the fingers in the position needed to hold the standard block.

4. A second block was given to the subject to hold for 10 seconds.

5. The subject was asked if the second block was longer, shorter, or the same length as the first block.

6. The procedure was repeated with each block in turn, until all the blocks had been tested.

The different blocks were not given to the subjects in any particular order apart from the standard block always being given to the subjects prior to a new block, so that the subject's responses were relative to the standard and not to any other block.

The results were recorded in a pre-designed table, as shown in the appendix - the following table is an abbreviated form of the results.

Numbers of musicians and non-musicians (out of 50) correctly identifying the differences in length of blocks of wood from a standard.

Block	Non-musicians	Musicians
A (+ 5 mm)	43	50
B (+ 2 mm)	27	39
C (standard)	-	-
D (- 2 mm)	16	39
E (- 5 mm)	41	50

6

Analysis of results

Since the results are of discrete data, i.e. numbers, I decided to use the χ^2 test for my analysis.

	Musicians	Non-musicians	TOTALS
A	50 (54.3)	43 (38.7)	93
B	39 (38.5)	27 (27.5)	66
D	39 (32.1)	11 (22.9)	55
E	50 (53.1)	41 (37.9)	91
TOTALS	178	127	305

χ^2 = $(50 - 54.3)^2/54.3$ + $(43 - 38.7)^2/38.7$ + $(39 - 38.5)^2/38.5$ + $(27 - 27.5)^2/27.5$ + $((39 - 32.1)^2/32.1$ + $(11 - 22.9)^2/22.9$ + $(50 - 53.1)^2/53.1$ + $(41 - 37.9)^2/37.9$ = **4.83**

Degrees of freedom $\quad$ = (rows minus one) $\times$ (columns minus one)
$\qquad\qquad\qquad\qquad$ = $(4 - 1) \times (2 - 1) = 3 \times 1 = 3$ df

Entering the table of χ^2 values at 3 degrees of freedom, with χ^2 equal to 4.83 gives us a value of p less than 0.2 but greater than 0.1. This indicates that there is no significant difference between the correct responses of the musicians and the non-musicians.

I suspected that the values for the blocks A and E which were 5 mm longer and shorter than the standard are not good enough discriminators, so I carried out a χ^2 test just for blocks B and D, i.e. those of just 2 mm difference from the standard block C.

The observed numbers of correct responses were as follows:

	MUSICIANS	NON-MUSICIANS	TOTALS
BLOCK B	39	27	66
BLOCK D	39	11	50
TOTALS	78	38	116

The expected numbers were calculated for each box:

	MUSICIANS	NON-MUSICIANS	TOTALS
BLOCK B	39 (44.4)	27 (21.6)	66
BLOCK D	39 (33.6)	11 (16.4)	50
TOTALS	78	38	116

The value for χ^2 was calculated as follows:

CELL	O	E	(O − E)	(O − E)^2	(O − E)^2/E
1	39	44.4	5.4	29.16	0.67
2	39	33.6	5.4	29.16	0.87
3	27	21.6	5.4	29.16	1.35
4	11	16.4	5.4	29.16	1.78

$$\chi^2 = 4.67$$

Degrees of freedom = $(c - 1) \times (r - 1) = 1 \times 1 = 1$

Entering the table of χ^2 at one degree of freedom, a value of 4.67 gives a p value <0.05 but >0.01, so I can conclude that the result is significant – there is a difference between the musicians and the non-musicians which is due to some factor other than chance.

However, when using one degree of freedom it is usual to apply Yates' correction factor whereby we subtract 0.5 from (O - E) before squaring. When this is done the χ^2 value is 3.82. This is just below the value of 3.84 which is that required for a p value of 0.05.

CONCLUSIONS

There was no significant difference in the ability of musicians and non-musicians to discriminate between the standard block of wood and those 5 mm longer or shorter. However, there was evidence to indicate that there was a difference with those blocks 2 mm shorter or longer than the standard Applying Yates' correction factor, although no significant difference was indicated, it was so close to significance that had I carried out the experiment with more subjects, I undoubtedly would have found a significant difference. If I had been able to produce blocks of even smaller differences in length, e.g. 1.5 mm or 1.0 mm, I think that the ability of musicians to tell these differences would have been even more significant. It is a pity that I do not have more time to refine the investigation and try it out.

From this investigation I have shown that musicians have a more highly developed kinesthetic sense than non-musicians.

SUGGESTIONS FOR FURTHER INVESTIGATIONS

1. Repetition of this investigation with a larger sample size.

2. Repetition of this investigation with smaller differences between blocks.

3. Kinesthetic ability in relation to age.

4. Kinesthetic ability in relation to gender.

5. Kinesthetic ability in relation to handedness.

BIBLIOGRAPHY

Beach, Lee Roy. *Psychology – Core Concepts and Special Topics*: Holt, Rhinehart and Winston. London, 1973.

Garvin, J.W. *Skills in Advanced Biology, Volume 1, Dealing with Data*. Stanley Thornes, Cheltenham, 1986.

Hill, Winifred F., *Learning*. Methuen and Co. London, 1963.

Neisser, Ulric. *Cognition and Reality*. W.H.Freeman and Co. San Francisco, 1976.

Wiseman, Stephen. *Intelligence and Ability*. Penguin. London, 1967.

ACKNOWLEDGEMENTS

I would like to take this opportunity of thanking:

My biology teacher, whose guidance and gentle (sometimes not so gentle) prodding was appreciated and necessary.

To all those subjects who participated willingly in the experiments.

To my fellow students, whose discussion at times over coffee could be less than helpful and assisted me to procrastinate.

To my parents who put up with me through it all.

APPENDIX

Raw data

Subject's reply coded as N = narrower, L = longer, S = same

NON-MUSICIANS	BLOCK				
	A	B	C	D	E
1	L	L	–	S	S
2	L	S	–	S	N
3	L	S	–	S	S
4	L	L	–	N	N
5	L	L	–	N	N
6	L	L	–	S	N
7	S	S	–	N	N
8	L	S	–	L	S
9	L	N	–	L	L
10	L	L	–	N	N
11	L	L	–	L	N
12	L	N	–	N	N
13	S	L	–	S	N
14	L	N	–	N	N
15	L	L	–	N	N
16	L	L	–	N	N

- Do the two projects differ in style? If so, in what ways do they differ?
- Which project write up do you prefer most, and why?
- Do you agree with the conclusions in each case?
- Suggest ways in which each of the investigations could be improved.

8 Suggestions for Investigations

We can divide most biology/human biology syllabuses and courses into the following eleven sections. I have listed some for each section which might be developed into interesting investigations, or may spark off some ideas of your own to follow up.

8.1 BASIC PRINCIPLES

▶ Diffusion, osmosis, etc. – for example, the rate of diffusion of dilute acid into gelatin blocks containing an indicator.
▶ Buffers – for example, the effect of adding acid to buffered and non-buffered solutions. Use of indicators, pH sensor, etc.
▶ Surface area/volume ratios in a variety of protists, plants and animals, including humans. For very tiny organisms like *Paramecium* micrometry can be used.

8.2 MOLECULES

▶ Many investigations can be based on carbohydrates, lipids, vitamins, enzymes, nucleic acids, etc. and their distribution in nature.
▶ Tests for these could be carried out on a variety of foods; manufacturers claims (on the label) could be tested.
▶ Techniques for separation of molecules – chromatography, dialysis, electrophoresis.
▶ There is a wide range of possible investigations with respect to enzymes, e.g. the effect of a range of factors on the rate of enzyme activity; the synthesis of starch from glucose-1-phosphate and potato enzyme extract – use of the colorimeter and conversion graphs.
▶ Browning in cut fruit and vegetables – the effect of temperature, pH, oxygen, etc.
▶ Starch digestion by a range of fungi using the starch agar well technique.
▶ The effect of bile salts on the rate of fat digestion by lipase – using agar wells.
▶ The vitamin C content of a variety of foods; cooked vs uncooked foods – using the DCPIP test.

8.3 CELLS

▶ The effect of temperature or solvents on the permeability of cell membranes using beetroot and colorimetry.
▶ Plasmolysis in onion cells – estimation of incipient plasmolysis – is it the same in different regions of the onion?
▶ Rates of contraction of the contractile vacuole in *Paramecium* in varying concentrations of the medium – microscopy.
▶ There are many possibilities for investigations using the microscope and micrometry – size of cells in different parts of an organism, e.g. an onion. Observation of the movement of chloroplasts in mosses.
▶ The distribution of cellulose, lignin, starch, etc. in different plant cells using appropriate stains.
▶ The distribution of cell organelles in different cell types; the size and number of cell organelles, e.g. mitochondria – use of electron micrographs.

8.4 MICROBIOLOGY

▶ Factors affecting the growth of bacteria, fungi, protozoa, yeasts – temperature, pH, moisture, substrate, etc.
▶ Antibiotic resistance in bacteria.
▶ Disinfectant concentration and bacterial growth.
▶ Food spoilage and its prevention.
▶ The keeping qualities of pasteurised and UHT milk compared with 'raw' milk.
▶ Making yoghurt.
▶ Alcohol tolerance in various species of yeast.
▶ Rate of fermentation/anaerobic respiration in yeast in relation to temperature, substrate, pH, etc. – use of the respirometer.

8.5 PHYSIOLOGY

Plants:

▶ Respiration in germinating seeds – use of respirometer – comparison of different types of food store, e.g. starch, oil.
▶ Comparison of transpiration rates: in different types of plant, under different environmental conditions – use of the potometer.
▶ Comparison of water loss and water uptake in deciduous and evergreen plants; xerophytes, mesophytes and hydrophytes, etc.
▶ Movement of eosin solution through celery, Busy Lizzie, etc.
▶ Water gain or loss by osmosis in, for example – plants/raisins/prunes/ potato cylinders/potato chips/dandelion scafes, etc.
▶ Water uptake in seeds, e.g. pea, broad bean, etc.
▶ Gaseous exchange in plants – relationship to light intensity; light frequency; concentration of carbon dioxide in atmosphere, etc – use of sodium hydrogen carbonate indicator and colorimeter.
▶ Photosynthesis – rate under various conditions.

- ▶ Pigment distribution in seaweeds and position on the shore.
- ▶ Chemical coordination in plants – the action of indole-acetic acid on stems and roots; effect of auxins on the growth of plant tissues or plant organs.
- ▶ The effect of respiratory inhibitors, oxygen, nitrogen, etc. on rate of ion uptake by carrot discs.
- ▶ The distribution of starch in plant storage organs.
- ▶ The distribution of starch in variegated dicotyledon leaves.
- ▶ The distribution of stomata in a variety of leaves; relationship to habitat.
- ▶ The effect of calcium chloride solution, sugar/salt solutions, light intensity or light frequency on stomatal aperture – use of micrometry.
- ▶ Flowering rhythm in a particular species of dicotyledon.

Animals:

- ▶ Water loss in woodlice, snails, etc.
- ▶ Water loss in relation to surface area: volume ratio.
- ▶ Coordination in animals – nervous and endocrine systems – walking in insects; responses of earthworms, turbellarians, etc.
- ▶ Comparisons of inspired and expired air in humans.
- ▶ Osmoregulation in a variety of animals – in freshwater, estuarine and marine environments.
- ▶ Respiration rates under varying conditions.

8.6 GENETICS AND EVOLUTION

- ▶ Root tip squashes and mitosis – in onion, crocus, broad bean, etc.
- ▶ Environmental conditions, e.g. temperature, pH, light intensity, etc. and their effect on mitosis.
- ▶ Duration of the stages of mitosis.
- ▶ Meiosis in *Hyacinthus*, *Tradescantia*, *Locusta* or grasshopper.
- ▶ Giant chromosomes in dipteran larvae.
- ▶ Starch production in wrinkled and round pea seeds.
- ▶ Estimation of owl prey by examination of owl faecal pellets.
- ▶ Analysis of feeding by the thrush by examination of anvil sites.
- ▶ Differential sexual selection of vestigial and normal winged *Drosophila*.
- ▶ Floral appearance under ultra-violet light.

8.7 GROWTH AND DEVELOPMENT

- ▶ The viability of pollen grains.
- ▶ Percentage germination of different types of seeds under various conditions.
- ▶ Seedling growth under various conditions.
- ▶ Dry mass determinations of oat seedlings.
- ▶ Growth of yeast in various media – use of haemocytometer.
- ▶ Growth of yeast under aerobic and anaerobic conditions.
- ▶ Fungal growth and temperature – measurement of mycelium diameter.
- ▶ Growth of yeast in different sugar substrates.

- Growth of bacteria in different culture media.
- Relative growth rates of maize and barley plants.
- Leaf area index for a crop plant.
- Growth in various insects.

8.8 BEHAVIOUR

- Mapping the human visual field.
- Plotting the fovea of the human eye.
- The extent of black and white, and colour vision in animals.
- Taxes and kineses in *Drosophila*, flatworms, beetles, woodlice, etc.
- Habituation in crawling snails.
- Homing behaviour in limpets.
- Courtship in tropical fish.
- Mapping the territories of birds, cats, etc.
- Peck order in chickens, cows, etc.
- Preference to a variety of conditions by woodlice (or other organism) using a choice chamber.
- Learning in animals – use of mazes.

8.9 ECOLOGY

- Inter- and intra-specific competition between plants.
- Predator–prey relationships – how they change over time.
- The distribution of insects in relation to plant cover – use of various traps.
- Population estimates of woodlice or other animals using capture/recapture techniques.
- Diversity indices of polluted and unpolluted streams, ponds, etc.
- Zonation of plants and animals on a rocky shore – use of transects, quadrats and point frames.
- The distribution of lugworms on a muddy/sandy beach.
- Comparison of plants and animals on exposed and sheltered coasts.
- Comparison of a particular characteristic of a plant or animal from an exposed and a sheltered coast.
- Succession on sand dunes – use of transects.
- Succession in newly uncovered soil over time.
- Survey of ponds, rivers, etc.
- Effect of pollution on the fauna and flora of a particular area.
- The effect of silage effluent on the growth of plants, e.g. *Lemna*.
- Shell colour in molluscs and temperature absorption.
- Dehydration in slug eggs.
- Rates of dehydration in seaweeds.
- Factors influencing the distribution of dandelion plants.
- Factors affecting the shape dandelion leaves.
- The efficiency of fruit dispersal.
- Biological indicators of pollution – lichens, tar-spot fungus on sycamore leaves.
- The use of fertilisers, herbicides, insecticides, etc.
- Food chains and food webs – use of artificial 'ponds'.

- A comparison of natural and artificial fertilisers on the growth of vegetables.
- The growth of tomatoes in growbags and ring culture.
- Comparison of vegetable yield in weeded and non-weeded plots.
- Mushroom growing – effect of temperature, moisture, compost, etc.
- Bread, cheese or yoghurt making.
- The coagulation of milk by rennin.
- Music and increased production of eggs by hens, milk by cows, etc.
- The effect of feeding on egg quality.
- A comparison of routine vs *ad libidum* feeding on chicken growth.
- The advantages of silage inoculants.
- The effect of wilting on silage effluent.
- The effect of density of sowing on crop production.
- The effect of soil compaction on crop production.
- The effectiveness of probiotics on the growth of pigs, calves, etc.
- Trout or salmon farming, e.g. growth rates, death rates, feeding, parasites, etc.

Useful addresses

BBC Education Information
White City
LONDON W12 7TS

ITV Education Television Company
PO Box 100
Warwick
CV34 6TZ

Answers and guide

This section gives the answers to questions asked throughout the book and offers suggestions where necessary.

2.2 A MODEL OF THE SCIENTIFIC METHOD

Page 10

1 The most common letters have more of them in a set.
The most common letters have the lowest values and vice versa.
All vowels have 1 point.

3.1 SAFETY

Page 25

1 Students should be 'tied' to a firm substrate by a strong line; they should also wear protective head-gear. They should always work in groups of at least two – certainly not alone.

3.3 MEASUREMENT

Page 31

1 (i) There is a 4 after the 7 so the answer is 46.7.
  (ii) There is an 8 after the 3 so the answer is 23.4.
  (iii) There is a 7 after the 9, so the 9 is rounded up to 10 – the answer is therefore 6.0.

Since the figure before the 5 is 3 and therefore odd we round *up* to 67.4.

Since the figure before the 5 is 8 and therefore even we round *down* to 66.8.

3.4 STANDARD FORM

Page 32

1 (i) Number between 1 and 10 = 2.5.
      Multiply 2.5 by 1000 or 10^3 to get to 2500.
      2500 in standard form is therefore 2.5×10^3.
  (ii) Number between 1 and 10 = 5.6.
      Divide by 1000 (i.e. 10^{-3}) to get back to 0.005 6.
      0.005 6 in standard form is therefore 5.6×10^{-3}.
  (iii) Number between 1 and 10 = 6.0.
      $6.0 \times 1\,000\,000\,(10^6) = 6\,000\,000$.
      In standard form = 6.0×10^6.
  (iv) $1.7 \times 10^{-5.}$
  (v) $2.338 \times 10^2.$
  (vi) $1.0 \times 10^3.$

Page 33

2 To divide powers of ten, subtract the powers.

3 (i) $841 = 8.41 \times 10^2$
      $0.003\,8 = 3.8 \times 10^{-3}$
      $262.4 = 2.624 \times 10^2$

Rewrite as $\dfrac{(8.41\times10^2)\times(3.8\times10^{-3})}{2.624\times10^2}$

Rearrange as $\dfrac{(8.41\times3.8)\times(10^2\times10^{-3})}{2.624\times10^2}$

$8.41 \times 3.8 = 31.958 = 3.195\,8 \times 10^1$

Rearrange as $\dfrac{3.195\,8}{2.624} \times \dfrac{(10^1\times10^2\times10^{-3})}{10^2}$

$3.195\,8 \div 2.624 = 1.217\,9$
$10^1 \times 10^2 \times 10^{-3} = $ (adding the powers they cancel out as 10^0)
Dividing by 10^2 means multiplying by 10^{-2}.
Answer $= 1.217\,9 \times 10^{-2}$

(ii) $0.000\,18 = 1.8 \times 10^{-4}$
$0.017 = 1.7 \times 10^{-2}$
$0.000\,006\,24 = 6.24 \times 10^{-6}$

Rewrite as $\dfrac{(1.8\times1.7)}{6.24} \times \dfrac{(10^{-4}\times10^{-2})}{10^{-6}}$

$= \dfrac{3.06}{6.24} \times \dfrac{10^{-6}}{10^{-6}}$

$= 0.490\,38$ and the 10^{-6}s cancel
now put $0.490\,38$ into standard form.
Answer $= 4.903\,8 \times 10^{-1}$

(iii) Rewrite as $\dfrac{(1.8\times3.76)}{4.8} \times \dfrac{(10^0\times10^2)}{10^{-1}}$

$= 1.41 \times 10^3.$

3.6 SAMPLING

Page 35

1 Anywhere there is a change of habitat or environment, for example:
- across sand dunes
- from the inside to the outside of a wood
- from a marshy to a dry area
- across a peat bog
- across a stream or pond
- across a well-trodden path.

Page 36

2 **a** – systematic (regular)
b – systematic (transect)
c – random
d – stratified random.

3 Disadvantages of **a** – although sampling using a regular grid does obtain samples from all parts of the population area, thus producing accurate estimates, this accuracy cannot be assessed and the data cannot be analysed statistically.

4 Transect – used where there is a physical or biological gradient.

5 Any information concerning the physical conditions along the transect, e.g. temperature, exposure time out of the water, salinity, trampling intensity, etc.

6 By definition of 'random' each sample should have an equal chance of

being selected. All statistical tests require that the data be collected randomly.

7 Stratified random techniques combine some of the advantages of **b** and **c**. The area under study is sub-divided and then each sub-division is randomly sampled. Each point in the area has therefore a greater chance of being sampled and the data are suitable for statistical analysis. This method is however, more time-consuming.

Page 38 Exercise (vi) t-test

$p<0.05$

There is a significant difference between the density of weeds in fields **A** and **B**. There is a greater density of weeds in field **A** therefore the herbicide has been effective.

Page 38 **8** Situation **b** is 'better' than **a** because a large number of small samples is more representative than a small number of large samples.

9 (i) **b** has the larger edge.
(ii) Difficulties in deciding whether any particular organism is included or not.
(iii) Random selection of quadrat positions.

Page 41 **12** Total number of points taken = $10 \times 50 = 500$

Total number of pins in contact = 244

% cover = $\dfrac{244}{500} \times 100 = 48.8\%$

3.8 CAPTURE–RECAPTURE

Page 43 **1** $84 \times \dfrac{102}{12} = 714$

3.9 EQUIPMENT

page 45 **1** $NaHCO_3$

Atomic mass of Na = 23, H = 1, C = 12 and O = 16

Molecular mass of $NaHCO_3$ = 23 + 1 + 12 + 48 = 84

1 litre of an M solution would contain 84 g

250 cm^3 of an M solution would contain $\dfrac{84}{4}$ = 21 g

250 cm^3 of an 0.25 M solution would contain $\dfrac{21}{4}$ = 5.25 g.

Page 48 **2** Read up the Y axis on the graph until you come to a colorimeter reading of 8; project across the graph until you intersect the graph line; project down to the X axis and read off the starch concentration.

3.10 LATIN SQUARES

Page 52 1 3 × 3 arrangement

A	B	C
B	C	A
C	A	B

5 × 5 arrangement

A	B	C	D	E
E	A	B	C	D
D	E	A	B	C
C	D	E	A	B
B	C	D	E	A

2

A	B	C		
	A	B	C	
		A	B	C
C			A	B
B	C			A

3 There are four types of leaf:
   A   100% green
   B   80–90% green
   C   50–80% green
   D   <50% green

There are four conditions:

1   no surfaces covered with jelly
2   top surface only covered
3   bottom surface only covered
4   both surfaces covered

For the types of leaf a latin square of 16 squares is required and 4 of these are required to cover the 4 conditions, as shown on the next page.

(3 cont.)

A1	B2	C3	D4	A4	B1	C2	D3
D1	A2	B3	C4	D4	A1	B2	C3
C1	D2	A3	B4	C4	D1	A2	B3
B1	C2	D3	A4	B4	C1	D2	A3
A3	B4	C1	D2	A2	B3	C4	D1
D3	A4	B1	C2	D2	A3	B4	C1
C3	D4	A1	B2	C2	D3	A4	B1
B3	C4	D1	A2	B2	C3	D4	A1

3.11 CONVERSION GRAPHS

Page 54

1 Height = 160 cm
Weight = 75 kg
Surface area = 1.8 m^2

Page 55

2 Kept going for 5 minutes
Pulse rate 60/30 secs
Fitness index = 100 (good)

3 Kept going for 3 minutes
Pulse rate 80/30 secs
Fitness index = 30 (very poor)

3.12 SURVEYS

Page 59

1 Suggested improvements:

(a) Tick the box which defines your age bracket

Under 20 ☐   20–29 ☐   30–39 ☐   40–49 ☐   Over 50 ☐

(b) Tick the appropriate box concerning the number of children you have:

None ☐   One ☐   Two ☐   Three ☐   Four ☐   Five or over ☐

(c) Tick the box which best describes your husband's income:
Under £15 000 per year ☐
£15 000–£20 000 ☐
£20 000 –£25 000, etc. ☐

(d) Which of the following tinned foods do you have in your house?
Baby foods ☐
Tinned fruit ☐
Tinned beans, etc ☐

Page 60

2 Sample of 100 in school of 1000, i.e. 1 in 10.
Stratified random sample would be best – representative of all ages.
Say there are 7 forms, i.e. about 14 in each form. Take a random sample of 14 from each form.

It doesn't say if it is a mixed school. If so, each sample of 14 should contain, say, 7 boys and 7 girls, again selected at random.

5.6 FORMULATING HYPOTHESES AND MAKING PREDICTIONS

Page 82   Each of the problems are given as testable hypotheses below.

1 Larger flowers have larger pollen grains than smaller flowers.

2 Wind-pollinated flowers make more pollen (as total mass) than insect-pollinated ones.

3 Pollen grains need sugar to grow. (The sugar could be specified, e.g. sucrose.)

4 No hypothesis – this is simply an analysis of nectar.

5 All seeds store starch as a food store.

6 All plants store starch in their leaves.

7 The larger a seed, the longer it takes to germinate.

8 Seeds germinate more quickly if they are frozen for two or three days.

9 Seeds germinate more quickly the longer they have been soaked beforehand.

10 Tomato 'pips' are more resistant to acid than apple 'pips'.

11 A dandelion 'clock' works.

12 The larger the surface area of a sycamore fruit the further it is dispersed.

5.8 EXERCISES IN THOUGHT EXPERIMENTS

Page 88 Exercise 1

i Acid rain slows down the rate of germination.

ii Whatever is readily available, e.g. cress or mustard seeds; pea or mung beans, etc.

iii Seeds on blotting paper in Petri dishes – 'damped' with different concentrations of sulphuric acid.

iv Series of dilute sulphuric acid after finding out the concentrations in acid rain – say five different concentrations. Some preliminary work will help in working out suitable concentrations – seeds should germinate within the range of concentrations.

5 Petri dishes for each concentration – so 25 dishes altogether.

10 seeds, all of the same type, in each Petri dish – 250 seeds in total.

Seeds evenly spaced in each dish on blotting paper. Each 'soaked' with the same volume of acid.

All dishes kept under the same conditions of temperature and in the dark.

v Numbers germinating for each concentration of acid – could convert to percentages – at different times, or after a given time. Could draw graph of percentage germinating against concentration of acid after given time.

vi Could calculate mean number and standard deviation germinating for each concentration – t test comparing two different concentrations.

Could use χ^2 – five categories (concentrations) and number germinating in each.

    i The percentages of homozygous dominants, heterozygotes and homozygous recessives of a particular trait in the sixth form.

    ii Select a particular trait which follows simple Mendelian monohybrid inheritance – that is, the gene has a dominant allele and a recessive allele (e.g. tongue-rolling or PTC tasting).

    iii Test all the students in the sixth form – whether they can roll their tongues or not, taste PTC or not, etc.

    iv Numbers able to roll/not roll tongues, taste/not taste PTC, etc.

    v Substitute the numbers appropriately in the Hardy-Weinberg equation to obtain numbers and thus percentages of homozygous dominants, heterozygotes and homozygous recessives.

    i A variety of hypotheses could be proposed. The 'home' sites are more readily found on the limestone. Since limpets rotate their shells so that they grind down the rock, and since limestone is much softer than basalt, limestone rocks are more obvious 'home' sites.

One hypothesis could therefore be: 'Limpets can find "homes" more readily on limestone than on basalt.'

    ii Select two areas, one of basalt and one of limestone, which are roughly the same in terms of exposure and which contain about the same numbers of limpets of the same species.

Without removing the limpets from their 'home' sites, give each one a unique mark (e.g. different combinations of colours and dots) using cellulose paint, which won't get washed off.

    iii Draw careful plans of the particular areas of basalt and limestone when uncovered by the tide, showing the positions of the 'home' sites.

Return when the limpets have been covered by the tide and then uncovered again.

Compare the position of limpets with the original plans to find out which limpets have returned to their 'home' sites.

    iv For each area of basalt and limestone the data will be numbers of limpets returning to their 'home' sites. These numbers can then be subjected to a suitable statistical test to determine if there is any significant difference between them.

Hypothesis – Adding onion juice to sugar solution prevents the growth of yeast.

Principles – Varying concentrations of onion juice are added to actively growing yeast cultures in a sugar medium. Growth of yeast measured using a haemocytometer.

Replicates and control (no onion juice added) required. All cultures with same sugar concentration and kept under the same environmental conditions.

Procedure – 5 replicates of yeast culture for each of 5 concentrations of onion juice. All 25 yeast cultures subdivided from original actively growing culture.

FIELD A

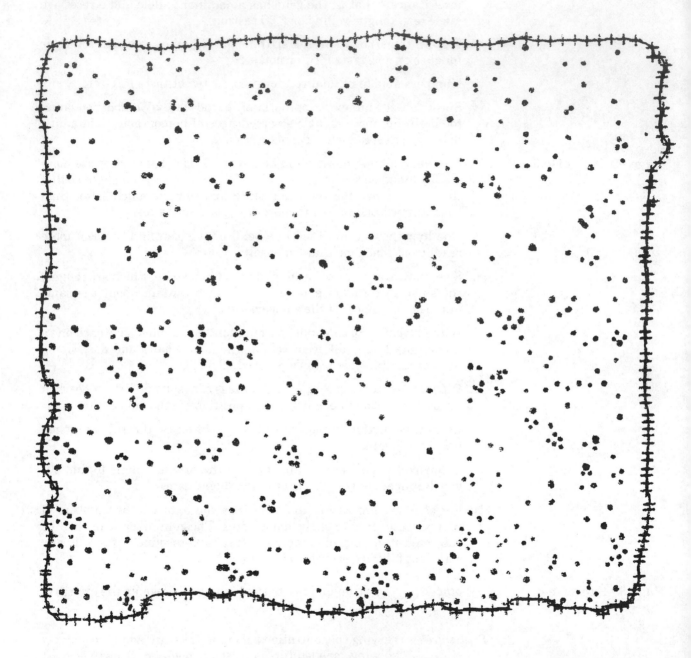

FIELD B

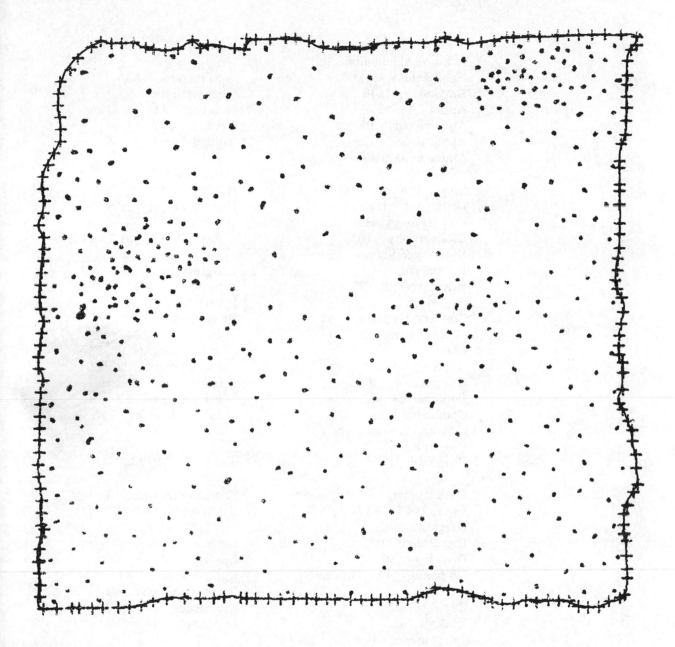

Index

- ▶ Soil analyses – air content, water content, humus content, pH, etc.
- ▶ Estimates of biomass.
- ▶ The effect of 'acid rain' on various plant processes.
- ▶ Population estimates of a particular organism in a defined area – plant or animal – use of a variety of appropriate techniques.
- ▶ The incidence of a particular parasite in a population.

8.10 HUMAN

- ▶ Variation in humans – height, mass, surface area, hand span, finger length, hearing, etc.
- ▶ The relationship between footsize and height in boys and girls.
- ▶ Distribution of tongue-rolling, ear lobe type, PTC tasting etc. in a particular population.
- ▶ Family trees with respect to eye colour, blood groups, skin colour, etc.
- ▶ Colour vision – comparison of males with females – use of Ishihara test.
- ▶ Measuring stress using blood pressure as a parameter – use of sphygmomanometer.
- ▶ The incidence of asthma attacks – conditions identified.
- ▶ Dental care and dental decay.
- ▶ Subcutaneous fat and skin fold measurements.
- ▶ Distance estimation – age, gender, etc.
- ▶ Laterality, e.g. handedness, eye dominance, etc.
- ▶ The effect of exercise on breathing – use of flow-rate meter.
- ▶ Differences between fit and unfit people – variety of tests.
- ▶ The incidence of respiratory disorders; heart disease, etc.
- ▶ The effect of regular exercise on the resting pulse rate.
- ▶ Pulse rate and age – use of data logging equipment.
- ▶ Fingerprint patterns of monozygotic and dizygotic twins.
- ▶ The effect of various stimuli on reaction times – light, sound, interference, touch, etc.
- ▶ Hair colour and water absorption.
- ▶ Hair colour and width of hair – use of micrometry.
- ▶ The incidence of athletes' foot, verruca, etc.
- ▶ Attitudes of people to controversial issues, e.g. smoking, drugs, pollution, ozone depletion, AIDS, genetic engineering, etc.
- ▶ A survey of slimming techniques and diets.
- ▶ Fibre, fats and food additives – surveys.

8.11 APPLICATIONS

- ▶ Skin protection products – how much UV light do they let through?
- ▶ The effectiveness of antibacterial mouthwashes.
- ▶ Extraction of fruit juice from apples using pectinase.
- ▶ Comparison of activity of immobilised and non-immobilised yeast cells, enzymes – use of sodium alginate beads.
- ▶ Comparison of biological and non-biological washing powders.
- ▶ Micropropagation – potatoes, cauliflower, African violet, carrot, etc.
- ▶ The effectiveness of rooting powders.
- ▶ The effectiveness of weed-killers – dose rate and efficiency.